The Life Story of Franklin Delano Roosevelt

A
COURAGEOUS
CONQUEST

by

MABEL MONTGOMERY

Edited by

HENRY I. CHRIST
Head of the English Department
Andrew Jackson High School
St. Albans, N. Y.

GLOBE BOOK COMPANY
NEW YORK, N. Y.

Grateful acknowledgement is herewith given to Tola Productions, Inc., for permission to use stills from its motion picture entitled "The Roosevelt Story."

FOREWORD

One of the chief factors in the success of a person's life is found in the choice of friends. Even when we have the will and the sense to choose friends well, we are limited by the narrow circle in which we move. However, there is no limit to the friendships we might form through books where "the great can talk to us as long as we like, whatever our rank or occupation, talk to us in the best words they can choose and of the things nearest their hearts."

Carlyle says that "the history of the world is but the biography of great men." And where better could young people find inspiration and stimulation than in reading true life stories of the men and women who have shaped destiny?

A COURAGEOUS CONQUEST is the life story of Franklin Delano Roosevelt, and even his political opponents will concede that an unbiased biography of him sketches the history of the United States from World War I until his death on April 12, 1945, compassing depression, recovery, wars, and almost peace. Many biographies have been written on Roosevelt for students of politics and government. But his rich life has remained a closed book to thousands because of the limitation of their vocabularies. A COURAGEOUS CONQUEST gives its readers a pen picture of Roosevelt, the humanitarian, in terms understandable to both the teen-ager and the adult. Dramatic episodes of the life of the late president are presented so as to inspire sympathy and emulation. It is the story of a lad unspoiled by riches, of a college student interested in campus leadership, of a young man crusading against machine politics, of a president who dared to accept and furnish leadership in a time of crisis, of a world leader fighting for peace, and of a gentleman who, having experienced personal disaster, believed in the dignity and rights of every individual.

The book is more than a biography. It includes an excellent

evaluation of his life as culled from the press at the time of his death as well as extracts from his speeches which are destined to take their place among the immortal addresses of the ages.

A COURAGEOUS CONQUEST should make every reader the friend of a man who will be listed among the great of all time.

WIL LOU GRAY, *Director, Opportunity School, South Carolina State Department of Education.*

PREFACE

"To strive, to seek, to find, and not to yield."

The line might well apply to Franklin Delano Roosevelt. Physically handicapped in a way that would discourage most men from tackling all but the simplest problems, Roosevelt aspired to the highest office in the land, and succeeded. He made an impression upon American and world history perhaps unequaled by any other American statesman.

If a man's stature is indicated by the stir he makes in the world, then F. D. R. was an eminent man indeed. No person in recent years has won more enthusiastic love and adulation; few persons in recent years have been objects of as much bitterness. His was no negative personality. Even his enemies conceded that he was a powerful, magnetic, positive leader of men.

The present book is long overdue. It attempts to present simply the fascinating story of Roosevelt's life. It attempts to show what the human spirit can endure and overcome. It is a paean to courage. It does not attempt a critical analysis of Roosevelt's place in history. The future will take care of that problem. It concentrates upon the undeniably remarkable aspects of his life, and leaves the controversies to the historians. The facts are here. His achievements are presented sympathetically; the man himself is interpreted with warmth and enthusiasm.

The book should be an inspiration to all people. Commonplace handicaps pale before the handicap that Roosevelt overcame. The lesson is clear. Not everyone can reach the White House; but everyone can try to conquer his own weaknesses and rise above handicaps.

The book is more than a biography of Roosevelt. It is a picture of life in America during the past few decades. It is a chart of our errors and our successes. It reminds us how far we have traveled since Roosevelt's death. It reminds us, when we most need reminding, of the roads to war. It emphasizes how important is the attempt to prevent war.

The book is a social document. In its emphasis upon Roosevelt's concern for the common man, it breathes the spirit of democracy. It reminds us that true democratic leadership is concerned with the plight of every citizen. It keeps us alert to the obligations of American leadership in the world.

The documents in Chapter 23 deserve serious study. They include some of the finest lines in the growing body of democratic literature. By themselves they provide an exciting panorama of a turbulent period. With the book they enrich the reader's understanding of Roosevelt and the world he helped to shape.

"If Roosevelt had lived . . ." Many Americans have wondered whether the world would be substantially different. Such conjecture is, of course, fruitless. Yet we can take heart from many of the statements that he left for us. The present book includes many of those sources of inspiration.

There is, then, a twofold gain for the readers of this biography. First, they are introduced to a dynamic personality —who is already becoming a legend. Secondly, they are given a brief account of American history at a crucial period. The period when Roosevelt lived is essential background for the events of today. Yet too often there is a wide gap between the last chapter in the history book and today's headlines. The present biography helps to fill part of the gap. It should encourage intelligent discussion of the citizen's place in world affairs, of the individual's responsibilities as well as privileges in modern society.

Readers of this book will be among those who will help to decide the fate of civilization under the shadow of the atomic and hydrogen bombs. The book is, we feel, a positive contribution to that breadth and understanding necessary for the securing of lasting peace.

HENRY I. CHRIST, *Editor*

CONTENTS

INTRODUCTION

Did you ever hear of illness doing anyone a good turn? That is what happened in the case of Franklin Delano Roosevelt. After his illness, he broke all American precedents by being elected President of the United States for one, two, three, and even four terms, though no other President had ever served more than two terms. Now about the illness. When he was thirty-nine years old and at the height of health and strength, his legs became helpless from infantile paralysis. The attack followed a swim in the chilly waters of the Bay of Fundy when he was overheated from a run across the island of Campobello, on the other side of which his summer home was situated.

Before this terrible calamity occurred, Franklin Roosevelt had been a superior athlete. Blessed with a fine mind and an excellent education, he possessed a splendid body as well. Because he felt so well, he had kept moving around constantly to provide an outlet for his tremendous energy. Tall, handsome, endowed with a happy family, abundant means and great personal charm, Mr. Roosevelt could expect life to hold every possible joy for him. The disaster changed entirely the face of things.

Without the least warning came the illness. At first he had to lie flat in bed for many long, weary months. As he improved, he was allowed to sit up, and finally he progressed to crutches. The doctors said he would never walk again. This medical opinion caused him to look forward to a future of helplessness as far as moving around on his own feet was concerned. He faced the black future with his usual courage and made up his mind never to ask for sympathy because of paralyzed legs. He was determined to be treated as a well man and to act that way as much as possible.

Though his legs had become helpless, his mind was keener and more active than ever before. Sitting still gave him a great deal of time to think. All the energy which he had formerly used up in physical activity was turned into thought. He thought about people who did not earn enough money on which to live properly. He thought about those who were hungry and could not find work. He thought about those suffering from ill health and poverty. He thought about people who were too old to work. He thought about those who lived in crowded city tenements and lonely farm cabins. He tried to think about ways of helping needy men, women and children to achieve more comfortable, more satisfying lives.

The illness was a turning point for Franklin Roosevelt. It matured him, made him leave youth behind. It gave him an understanding of the burdens of others which he might otherwise never have had. When he became President on March 4th, 1933, his own fight to overcome paralysis gave him the courage to fight social and economic evils and to keep on fighting until the evils were somewhat remedied.

President Roosevelt was very happy over the improvement in the living conditions of the American people. He was happy because his fight for the "forgotten man" had been partially successful, and he wanted the improvement to continue. His desire was to build a better world and he had no idea of stopping short of his goal. Perhaps he took as his motto the famous words of his boyhood hero, Captain John Paul Jones, "I have just begun to fight!" Certainly he did not mind a good fight in order to get what he thought people needed and should have. He believed that national prosperity depended on raising the standard of living for all the people and not just for a few. He wanted the good things of life to be shared by all.

He was not afraid to try new ways of doing things. Someone has said that his motto was, "Try it!" He once stated in a speech in Atlanta, "It is common sense to take a method and try it. If it fails, admit it and try another, but, above all, *try something!*"

Then on December 7th, 1941, the Japanese attacked Pearl Harbor and the United States entered World War II. Because of his previous experienced leadership in national affairs as President of the United States, Mr. Roosevelt soon became an acknowledged world leader. He showed the same fearless courage in fighting for the rights of the common man all over the world, and for the rights of small nations, that he had shown in helping "the forgotten man" in the United States. He felt that every human being was entitled to the "four freedoms"—freedom of speech, freedom of religion, freedom from want, freedom from fear—and he hoped that these basic freedoms would come to all people following the war.

When Franklin D. Roosevelt died April 12th, 1945, he was mourned by people of other races, who live in far-off countries around the globe, as well as by inhabitants of the United States.

He lived vigorously and courageously. He died valiantly, a war casualty as surely as if he had given his life in combat duty.

No one knows how he will be judged by the passing of time. That remains to be decided by the future. But several things are certain. He showed that in time of stress it is the duty of the government to care for its *people* as well as its *resources*. He, like Lincoln, placed people above property. Long before the United States entered World War II, he had championed the cause of freedom in the democratic nations fighting for their existence. He broke the American tradition that no president should be elected for more than two terms, and his understanding leadership, especially during World War II, justified the breaking of the precedent. He was the friend of the 130,000,000 inhabitants of the United States as well as the friend of depressed and liberty-loving people everywhere.

If this little book helps you to know him as boy, man, governor, president, and acknowledged world-leader, the author will be more than happy.

MABEL MONTGOMERY

CHAPTER ONE

CHILDHOOD

January 30th, 1882, was an important day to· Mr. and Mrs. James Roosevelt, for on that day a son, Franklin Delano, was born to them at their beautiful estate near Hyde Park, New York. The date is an important one to the United States since the little boy who came into the world on that cold January day broke all American precedents by being elected and re-elected President four times. During his presidency, each year his birthday was celebrated with many huge balls held all over the nation, and the money derived from the balls was used for crippled children. When he was born, his parents had no idea that his birthday would later become a national event or that he would in time be a world-leader.

Mr. and Mrs. Roosevelt were delighted over the arrival of Franklin. Of course they did not realize that some day he would be President. Mrs. Roosevelt's ambition for her son was a very different one from that. She wanted him to grow up to be exactly like his father, an honorable, kind, just American. She lived to see him become all that and President, too!

Except for a grown-up half brother, Franklin was an only child. When his father was a widower fifty-two years old, he married Sarah Delano, a tall, handsome young woman almost half his age. They were neigh-

1

bors. The Delanos lived not far from Hyde Park on the opposite side of the Hudson River. The Roosevelt family had lived in Dutchess County for a long time, ever since Isaac Roosevelt came to Dutchess for his bride during the French and Indian wars, probably about 1756. The Roosevelts had been in New York State an even longer time. The Roosevelt family is one of the oldest in the United States, and the name Roosevelt, translated from Dutch into English, means "a field of roses." The first Roosevelt, whose name was Claes, came to America from Holland in 1644 and settled in New Amsterdam, the present New York City. From the time of that first settler, the Roosevelts have been people who have owned property and money, have been well educated and have stood high in their community. Another Roosevelt, Theodore, a cousin of Franklin's, was President thirty-two years before Franklin.

Franklin's parents named him for an uncle of Mrs. Roosevelt's. He was a plump, smiling, happy baby, always in cheerful humor. As he grew, he became a very handsome child, with large blue eyes and a mop of fair, curly hair. Everyone who saw him remarked about his unusually good appearance.

Mr. and Mrs. Roosevelt had enough money so that they did not have to worry about how and where they would live. They did not throw money away, though they lived in comfort and surrounded their son with everything good. Because they idolized Franklin, their great love made them anxious to bring him up wisely and not to spoil him. They loved the country them-

Franklin Roosevelt as a handsome boy.

selves; they thought it a better place in which to live than New York City, seventy miles away. They wanted Franklin to love the country, too. Though Mr. Roosevelt had many business interests in New York City, he and Mrs. Roosevelt decided to make Hyde Park their permanent home. Franklin was brought up in the big, rambling old house which today is a national shrine and which stands on the top of a steep wooded hill overlooking the Hudson River. It was up this same river that Hendrik Hudson, another Dutchman, had sailed many years before. This house, built about 1750, was bought and remodeled by Mr. James Roosevelt because he wanted to live near the river. A view down the Hudson for miles may be seen from the windows of the library. Fine old trees and evergreen shrubs surround the house. A brook gurgles through the near-by woods. In fall and winter, when the trees are bare of leaves, a glimpse of the house may be caught from the highway.

Though Franklin was an only child, he was not lonely. His father and mother made him their constant companion. There were, besides, many relatives and neighbors. Merry young cousins came to Hyde Park; Edmund Rogers, Franklin's chum, lived not far away.

Once a tiny girl cousin arrived for a visit with her father. Anna Eleanor was her name. Only a year and a half old, she seemed very small to Franklin, who was four. He rode her around the nursery on his back, and not a soul dreamed that when Franklin grew up he would marry Anna Eleanor.

When he was five years old another interesting event

happened. His father took him on a trip to Washington. They went to the White House to call on President Grover Cleveland, a close friend of Mr. James Roosevelt. President Cleveland patted small, handsome Franklin on the head.

"I am making a strange wish for you, my little man," said President Cleveland. "It is a wish no one else is likely to make. I wish that you may never become President of the United States."

President Cleveland made that wish because being President of the United States is a very hard job. But his statement did not discourage small Franklin.

The days at Hyde Park were full of interests for a growing boy. Mrs. Roosevelt believed that a person, however young, was much happier if kept constantly busy. There were certain hours for Franklin to eat, hours for him to play, hours for him to study, hours for him to be read to. No one realized that such a set routine irritated Franklin until one day, when he was about five years old, he became very much depressed. Nothing amused him. His mother tried to find out the trouble.

"Are you unhappy?" she asked.

"Yes," replied Franklin.

"Why are you unhappy?" she further inquired.

"Oh, for freedom!" cried Franklin, much to his mother's surprise, for that was such an odd speech for a little boy to make.

Mr. and Mrs. Roosevelt talked the matter over, as they did everything relating to Franklin. They decided to let him try freedom for one day. Next morning he was told that he could do exactly as he pleased. All day long no one told him it was time to bathe, eat, play or study. He was absolutely free.

That night a dirty, tired little boy came home. No one asked where he had been or what he had done. One day of freedom must have been enough, for the next morning he went back to his set routine very cheerfully, and was content to follow it from that time on.

Franklin wanted pets. Mr. and Mrs. Roosevelt were quite willing for him to have them, but they believed that he should be responsible for them. When he was five, his uncle, Warren Delano, gave him a dog, a beautiful red Irish setter named Marksman. His father and mother let him accept Marksman on the condition that he would care for Marksman himself. Marksman followed Franklin everywhere, and they had a great deal of fun playing together. After every meal Franklin would take food down to the barn for Marksman; he knew that Marksman would go hungry unless he fed him.

When Franklin was seven, his father bought him a pony on the same terms, that he must take care of it himself. He kept his word faithfully. At first he looked too little to sit on top of the pony. After awhile he became a good enough rider to have a small horse instead of the pony, and to ride at the Dutchess county fair.

Franklin did not go to the public school. He had private teachers at home. At first his teachers were women; when he was nine, he was tutored by a man.

Books filled the house at Hyde Park. Mr. and Mrs. Roosevelt did not choose the books for Franklin to read but preferred that he select his own books. He liked to read history, particularly naval history, better than anything else.

His love of reading did not interfere with his love of games and sports. He was very active and restless, and had hobbies which changed according to his age and the season of the year. Edmund Rogers and he swam, climbed trees, dug caves, built boats, ice-skated, collected stamps, and indulged in many other kinds of fun. Whatever he did, he did with zest. He always enjoyed himself thoroughly.

One of his hobbies, which continued throughout his life, was collecting stamps. During his mother's childhood she had lived in China and collected foreign stamps. She turned her collection over to Franklin. He added to it until it was considered very fine.

Child-like, he always wanted to win every game he played. When he was very small, he usually played with his Scotch nurse, who let him win. His mother did not consider that method proper training for life. Once he asked his mother to play a game of steeple-chase with him. His mother's horse won. He insisted on "swapping horses" for the next game. His mother agreed, and she won again. This made him angry. His mother took the horses away and told him he could not play that game, or any other game, until he learned to take a beating in good temper. Perhaps this early lesson may account for the fact that he became a good loser.

He had a way of ordering his playmates around, and they generally permitted him to do so. His mother felt that this was neither wise nor right. She said to him, "My son, don't give the orders all the time. Let the other boys give them sometime."

"Mummie," he answered seriously, "if I don't give the orders, nothing will happen!"

CHAPTER TWO

BOYHOOD

There were five hundred acres of land in the Roosevelt estate, which gave plenty of room for Franklin to roam and play. Many trees grew on the land. Mr. Roosevelt loved trees and would never let a tree be cut unless it was decayed. He also planted many young trees. Franklin could climb like a squirrel and liked to do so. The taller the trees were, the better he liked them. Edmund Rogers and he built a sailboat in the top of a hemlock tree. Mrs. Roosevelt felt uneasy for fear the boys would fall out and tumble to the ground, but they did not. Like tree-sitters of later days, they sat in their boat high among the waving green branches, looked clear across the wide Hudson River and played that they were sailing distant seas.

After a day of playing, riding or climbing he enjoyed coming home to a cheery fire burning in the library fireplace. Franklin would lie on the rug before the fire, in the book-lined room, and read and dream. Perhaps he dreamed of beating Edmund Rogers at sailing boats next day. Perhaps he dreamed of being president some day. Perhaps he dreamed of making people happy.

From his earliest years Franklin wanted to shoot. At first he had a bow and arrow, but this did not satisfy him. A real gun was what he wanted. His father let him have a gun before his mother was willing, and he was a crack shot at eleven years. He did not kill uselessly but because he wished to establish in his home a museum which would contain one of each kind of the Hudson River birds—to be shot by himself. He even learned to mount the birds for his museum. They are still in the Hyde Park house.

Mrs. Roosevelt said that she never worried about Franklin when he was away from her. She and his father tried to teach him to amuse himself, to think things out for himself, to depend on himself and to decide for himself. They had confidence in his judgment and felt sure that he would not start anything which he could not finish. Mr. and Mrs. Roosevelt also never said unnecessary "don'ts" to Franklin. His father believed in keeping Franklin's mind occupied with interesting things. Franklin did not realize he was being directed or following any idea but his own.

Everything about the sea thrilled Franklin very early. John Paul Jones was his special hero. This love of the sea came from Mrs. Roosevelt's side of the family. Her grandfather had owned fast clipper ships that sailed all over the world. Her father, Mr. Delano, had business interests in China. When Mrs. Roosevelt was a little girl, her mother, with the entire family of small children, sailed to China to join Mr. Delano. Then the voyage around Cape Horn took four long months. The Delanos lived in China for awhile, returning home through Europe.

They spent one winter in France and another in Germany. With her brothers and sisters, Mrs. Roosevelt went to school in each country. She learned to speak French and German fluently. Because she enjoyed traveling, she wanted Franklin to learn geography, history and languages by traveling. Mr. and Mrs. Roosevelt began taking Franklin to Europe with them when he was very young. From the time he was seven until he was fifteen, Franklin spent several months abroad each year. A different European country was visited on each trip.

When Franklin grew older, he and his tutor traveled together while Mr. and Mrs. Roosevelt remained at one place. During two summers, Franklin and the tutor rode through Germany and Switzerland on bicycles. The first summer, each of them had an allowance of four marks ($1.00) a day. This meant that they had to live very cheaply, eating black bread and cheese, and sleeping in peasants' homes or small country inns. When Franklin rejoined them at Nauheim, Germany, Mr. and Mrs. Roosevelt were very much surprised to find that he had saved a large amount of the money. On the same trip Franklin was also able to get himself and the tutor out of several amusing situations by the ease with which he spoke German.

However, the sea continued to be Franklin's passion. He read all the naval history he could find, and wanted to enter Annapolis. His father had other ideas for his son. Mr. Roosevelt wanted Franklin to be able to take over his own business interests and not become a sailor. A good general education seemed the best preparation for the life Franklin would lead. Mr. Roosevelt felt that an excellent boys' preparatory school, followed by

Harvard University and a law school would be best. Mr. Roosevelt talked the matter over with Franklin as one man to another, because that was the way he always discussed everything with Franklin. As a compromise for giving up the idea of Annapolis, his father gave him a twenty-one foot sailboat.

CHAPTER THREE

EDUCATION

When Franklin was fourteen, Mr. and Mrs. Roosevelt took him to Groton, a preparatory school. Along with them went Mr. and Mrs. Rogers and Edmund. The four parents left two homesick boys behind them. The parting was almost as hard on the parents as on the boys.

At Groton, a brand new world opened to Franklin. For the first time he was away from his parents, among boys of his age, and "on his own." Most of the boys in his class had already been at school for two years. It was only natural that they might resent a new boy. However, Franklin was so friendly and had such a winning smile for everybody, that he soon made many friends. His years of traveling stood him in good stead. The traveling had accustomed him to meeting new people constantly; therefore, he did not mind the strangers at school. They soon became his friends.

His traveling also helped in another way. He could speak both French and German with as much ease as a native of either country. His studies were easy for him. He liked debating and became a member of the school debating team. The members of the team debated many crucial subjects, such as "Should Capital Punishment Be Abolished?" or "Should the United States Navy Be Increased?" These early debates helped

13

At Groton School football, baseball, rowing, and cross-country running were favorite sports with Franklin, center. Whether he won or lost had little effect on his enthusiasm.

to develop his skill as a speaker and a keen thinker. Franklin threw himself into games as well as studies. Football, baseball, rowing and cross-country running were favorites. He played baseball well and was man-

14

ager of the team. His unusual height helped him make a record for the running high kick at seven feet, three and one-half inches. This record remained unbroken for years. Whether he won at what he undertook, or whether he lost, it had little effect upon his enthusiasm. He was a good sport always.

Because he had been kept away from other children, Franklin had missed the usual childish illnesses. At Groton, he promptly made up for lost time by having them all. While he was suffering from scarlet fever, his mother could not visit him unless she agreed to be shut up in the room with him. She got around the rule by climbing a rickety ladder outside his window. Every day she would perch on top of the wobbly ladder and, through this open window, talk to Franklin in bed. Her daily visits, by means of the ladder, cheered and amused Franklin until he was well.

Another illness may have prevented a great change in Franklin's life. He had always longed to be a sailor. The Spanish-American War in 1898 revived his former desire to enter the Navy. Franklin and another boy planned to run away to Boston and enlist in the Navy for service in Cuba. Twice a week a pieman came to the school to sell pies and cakes. They arranged to ride with this pieman, well hidden in the bottom of his cart, to the nearest railroad station five miles away. Both the boys were unusually tall and looked older than their sixteen years. They might have gotten miles distant, perhaps have been accepted by the Boston Navy office and on their way to Cuba, before the school authorities found out. But luck was against their becoming sailors. The night before they were to leave, both of them were sick. Next morning, which was to have been *the* morning of the great adventure, they awoke with running noses, sore throats and splitting headaches. They were ashamed to find that they had measles! They were therefore kept in bed at school like little boys, and they could not run away to join the Navy.

After Franklin's several illnesses, his mother was strongly tempted to coddle him. She would have liked to take him home to Hyde Park to get well, where she could have fed and petted him to her heart's content, or to have paid him frequent visits. She put both temptations behind her and let him remain at school because she felt that it was better for him to remain there.

The Groton allowance for spending money for each boy was fixed at twenty-five cents a week. Even if a boy were rich, he could have no more. Of the twenty-five cents, ten cents had to go in the collection plate at church each Sunday; the remaining large sum of fifteen cents was his to do with as he pleased. Like all the other boys, Franklin had to live within his allowance.

After a year of study, Franklin rejoiced when summer holidays drew near. While at Groton, he sometimes attended summer camps which were run by the school. More often he spent his vacations at Campobello, an island two miles off the coast of Maine, where the Roosevelts had a summer cottage. Here Franklin indulged his love of the sea. With his twenty-one foot boat, he explored the coast and learned a great deal about running a boat. Sometimes he was late getting home from the trips. Fogs occasionally delayed him. Most mothers would have worried when night came and a young son was still out in his boat. His mother said that she did not worry. She believed, as she did when he was younger, that he would not undertake anything he could not finish. She felt sure that he knew how to sail a boat, that he would not run any undue risk, and would return safely. He always did.

Franklin graduated from Groton with honors. He was a tall fair boy, with keen blue eyes, a firm chin and a happy smile. In the fall of 1900, at the age of eighteen years, he entered Harvard University at Cambridge.

Exactly three months afterward, Mr. Roosevelt died. Even though there was a great difference in their ages, Franklin and his father had been chums, so his death was a severe blow. This sorrow made Franklin feel older, sadder, and more of a man.

Mr. Roosevelt's death left Mrs. Roosevelt very lonely. She did not want to live alone in the big house at Hyde Park. In order to be near Franklin, she rented a house in Boston, but she was careful not to interfere with his college life.

Mrs. Roosevelt's rented Boston house became the week-end center for Franklin and his friends. This gave his mother the pleasure of having gay young people around her. She seldom visited Franklin's rooms at Harvard. Though she was in the same city with him,

Franklin, with his father and mother, about the time he graduated
from Groton School. He was then a tall, fair boy with keen blue eyes,
a firm chin and a happy smile.

she went to his rooms only when he invited her for some special occasion, for she believed that mothers should not be in evidence at college.

Since Franklin's parents were wealthy, he naturally selected as his living quarters those provided for rich boys. However, he was no snob. He made friends not only with his own group but with boys who worked their way through college. His classmates found him full of energy and enthusiasm. He possessed great personal charm, which he always retained in strong measure. Naturally, he was a leader among his fellow students. In fact, he could get the students to do almost anything he wanted done. He had delightful manners. He attended dances and social parties, but he was not a ladies' man. Sometimes he took a tall, fair girl, named Anna Eleanor Roosevelt, to football games, but nobody thought anything of that. Wasn't she his cousin?

His love of American naval history led him to specialize in American political history and government. Besides his studies, his college interests were extensive. He was one of the most active members of the Political Club, which brought public men to Harvard to talk and lead discussions. Franklin's classmates were astonished to find that he was a Democrat and stood for Bryan, who was running for the presidency on the Democratic ticket, rather than for McKinley, the Republican candidate. This seemed surprising to the other young men because Theodore Roosevelt, Franklin's distant cousin, wanted to be Vice-President under McKinley on the Republican ticket. Theodore's name was constantly in the papers. It was hard for Harvard young men to realize that all Roosevelts might not belong to the same political party. The Harvard men did not know that originally all the older Roosevelts had been Democrats. Franklin's father, as well as Theodore's father, entered the Republican party during the Civil War. Theodore's father remained a Republican while Franklin's father came back to the Democratic party.

The Crimson, the college newspaper, written and published by the students, became Franklin's strongest college interest outside his classes. He started on *The Crimson* as a cub reporter and hunted hard for news items which might have escaped the attention of the more experienced editors. Once he found out that his cousin Theodore was coming to visit the president of Harvard and ran that item, which the president of Harvard did not want known. In his sophomore year he was one of several editors, later becoming editor-in-chief. He relished writing red-hot editorials about college matters. Some of his editorial subjects were "Poor Sportsmanship," "The Weak Volume of Cheering at Games," and what he considered lack of proper measures for the prevention of fires. He kept on the last subject so hard that his editorials finally led to the installation of fire escapes in the dormitories. He praised as strongly as he criticized severely. This trait of honesty earned for him the reputation of being fair and just in what he wrote.

Sports still interested Franklin as much as ever. Among the thousands of fine young men at Harvard, it was harder to be rated a star at athletics than it had been at Groton. Franklin did not become a tennis champion, a football hero, or make the varsity rowing team. He enjoyed these activities personally even if he did not reach the top in any of them. Perhaps he might have suffered disappointment owing to his failure to become an athletic star if he had not had so many interests to occupy him.

One of these interests was collecting books. As the Navy had always been a hobby of his, he began to collect books on naval history. Very often he could be found in Boston's old second-hand book shops hunting for rare books about the Navy. He continually added to his early library until at the time of his death he owned a remarkable collection of books and old prints on naval subjects.

Summer vacations were usually spent at Hyde Park and Campobello. When at Hyde Park, he invited his friends to visit him at the same time that the Rogers boys brought their friends home from Yale. There were games and picnics during the day and dances every night. A gay house party would soon be under way. At Campobello, a larger boat, the *Half Moon,* had taken the place of the earlier, smaller one. In the *Half Moon* Franklin sailed on several adventures, exploring the coast which he loved.

He graduated from Harvard in three years instead of the usual four. However, he remained for a fourth year, during which he took graduate work in government, politics and sociology. The next fall he entered the law school at Columbia University, New York City. He also announced his engagement to his distant cou-

Franklin and his mother during his student days at Harvard where he graduated in three years instead of the usual four.

sin, Anna Eleanor Roosevelt, the same little girl, now tall and fair, whom he had ridden on his back in the nursery at Hyde Park years before.

Because her parents had died during her childhood, Eleanor had lived with her grandmother Hall, her mother's mother. As she grew up, she had attended an excellent school, supervised by a Frenchwoman, in England, and had traveled in Europe for further education. Because of her staying abroad so much, she had seen little of Franklin. In fact, her grandmother Hall thought it just as well if Eleanor did not see too much of those energetic Roosevelts! When Eleanor was fifteen, her aunt gave a dance at her home in New York City. There was Franklin, handsome and gay and sure of himself. Eleanor's mother had been beautiful, her aunts were beautiful, and Eleanor was not even pretty. This caused Eleanor to be shy and to feel that she was an awkward dancer. When Franklin asked her to dance with him the night of the party, her cup of joy overflowed. He did not find her a poor dancer. His admiration for her gave her more confidence in herself.

From that time they were often together. No one thought anything of it because they were cousins. Franklin kept his love affair to himself. Not even his roommate at Harvard shared the secret until he had a letter from Franklin telling the wonderful news of the engagement just before it was made public.

CHAPTER FOUR

MARRIAGE AND EARLY MANHOOD

The following spring, on March 17th, 1905, Franklin and Eleanor were married at the home of her aunt in New York City. He was twenty-three and she twenty. Theodore Roosevelt, the President of the United States, gave away the bride, who was his niece. Franklin's mother said she would never forget "how straight and strong and glowing the children looked during the ceremony." The bride and groom always insisted that they played second fiddle at their own wedding and were far less important to their guests than President Theodore Roosevelt. Just as the ceremony started, the Irish, parading because it was St. Patrick's Day, passed along outside the house singing "The Wearing of the Green." They sang so lustily, in honor of the President, that their voices almost drowned out the words which were making Franklin and Eleanor man and wife.

As soon as the law school ended in June, Franklin and Eleanor went abroad for a wedding trip. When they returned, the first thing they did was to set about starting a home of their own. They rented a tiny house, just twelve feet wide, but several stories tall, in 36th Street, New York City. The house was so small it seemed almost a doll house, but out of it Anna Eleanor Roosevelt made a real home. Franklin had his treasured naval books and pictures around him. Both

Franklin and his cousin Eleanor Roosevelt were married on March 17, 1905.

liked to have their friends for meals and entertained as much as they could without interfering with Franklin's studies.

At the end of Franklin's second year at law school a little girl was born to the Franklin Roosevelts. She was given her mother's name, Anna Eleanor. Mrs. James Roosevelt, a proud grandmother, said that the baby was golden haired and had deep blue eyes which laughed very often.

The young couple continued to live in New York. Week-ends and vacations were spent at Hyde Park, which they loved. There they played golf and tennis, swam and looked after the estate. The forestry end of the farm interested Franklin very much indeed. He continued to plant young trees as his father had done. He knew that trees prevented soil erosion and helped control floods as well as gave a yearly crop if properly cut.

He followed in his father's footsteps in other ways too, gradually taking his father's place in the country life around Hyde Park. He became, among other things, a member of a volunteer fire company, a school trustee, and a director of the First National Bank of Poughkeepsie. He liked to talk politics with the older residents of the village of Hyde Park.

CHAPTER FIVE

POLITICS

After he was admitted to the bar, Franklin entered a New York law firm. It was natural that he and his wife should see a good deal of her uncle, President Theodore Roosevelt, who constantly urged that it was the duty of young men to enter politics, an idea which appealed to Franklin. He had always been interested in public matters, and he enjoyed arguing about them. But he was beginning to get a good law practice, so he put away the thought of public life as something for the future.

The nomination for the state senatorship from his district was suddenly offered him. He was urged to run as a patriotic duty. There seemed no possible chance that a Democrat could win; only one Democratic senator from that district had been elected since 1856. Franklin did not, at first, want to waste time in running when he was certain of defeat. He thought the matter over for a day and night and at last agreed to run. He decided to make it a real race and threw himself into the fight with his whole heart and soul, as he plunged into everything. The time before the election was very short. Most candidates used horses and buggies for getting around, but he decided that that means of travel was too slow for his purpose. He decided to call personally on every voter, if possible. In

those days automobiles were new, as well as uncertain,
but he bought an open single-seated Maxwell car,
painted it red, and named it the Red Peril. The Red
Peril saved time. In it he raced through the countryside, delivering speeches from town halls, public
squares, apple orchards, and sometimes from the tops
of haystacks. He stopped farmers in the fields to talk
to them. He stopped workmen along the roads. He
used every chance to meet people and get votes prom-
ised to him. To his own surprise, and to the great surprise of the party leaders, he was elected. Thus he
started along the way which led to the Presidency,
though no one realized it at the time.

The news of his election reached Big Tim Sullivan,
the leader of Tammany Hall, a powerful political organization in New York City.

Big Tim said, "You know these Roosevelts. This
fellow is still young. Wouldn't it be safer to take him
out and drown him before he grows up? If you don't,
he'll cause trouble sure as shootin' before he's much
older."

Franklin had made up his mind to be independent,
if elected.

In his speech accepting the nomination, he said,
"As you know, I accept the nomination with absolute
independence. I am pledged to no man; I am influenced
by no interests; and so I shall remain. If elected, I
will give my entire time to serving the people of this
district."

Most of the members of the legislature who came to
Albany, the capital of New York, lived in hotels, going

home for week-ends. The Franklin Roosevelts decided that the making of laws should be a full-time job. They rented a house in Albany and on January 1st, 1911, moved themselves and their small children into it. On the first day of the session, the newspaper men wrote of Franklin as the "baby" of the senate; they praised his good looks, but they knew nothing of his keen mind.

Franklin soon showed that he meant it when he had said he would be independent. He organized a small band of fellow legislators to defeat the election of a man who, he felt, was unsuited to become a member of the United States Senate. This act brought Franklin to the attention of the public, and much pressure was brought to cause him to give in and surrender. The battle raged more than three months. How Franklin enjoyed it! The Roosevelt house was the meeting place of his small and courageous group of followers. Mrs. Roosevelt helped by fitting up a room in the house for their use. They enjoyed meeting there. The men stuck solidly behind Franklin until they won. The victory, his first in public life, showed how well he could organize a group and how he could hold the men together. Young Senator Roosevelt was much praised for his success.

An older member of the legislature, named Alfred E. Smith and known as "Al" to everybody, had had far more experience in practical politics than had Franklin Roosevelt. By his own efforts, Al Smith had come up from the sidewalks of New York City while Franklin Roosevelt had been born and reared in luxury. Though greatly different, the two men liked each other. Al Smith gave good advice to the young senator from Dutchess County, and the two became warm friends. Another friend whom he made was Louis Howe, a newspaper man.

Franklin found one term in the senate a very interesting experience. At the end of the term he felt that he should give up politics and return to the practice of law. Of course, the political bosses whom he had fought and beaten were delighted at this prospect. When he heard of their joy at his leaving, he promptly changed his mind and ran again. Though he was unable to run in person because he was ill with typhoid fever, this campaign gave him even more votes than the first. Louis Howe managed it for him. He returned to Albany for a second term in the senate of New York State.

In the meantime, national politics was exciting. Franklin admired Woodrow Wilson very much and did his share in electing Wilson to the Presidency, the first Democrat to hold that high office since Grover Cleveland.

CHAPTER SIX

ASSISTANT SECRETARY OF THE NAVY

Franklin was immediately offered a place as Assistant-Secretary of the Navy in the Wilson administration. His strong love of ships and the sea caused him to accept at once. He resigned as state senator and on March 17th, 1913, his wedding anniversary, he took the oath of office. He was only thirty-one years of age, the youngest man ever to hold the job.

He and his wife rented a small Washington house, into which they moved, with the three children and servants. In spite of many social invitations, the Franklin Roosevelts continued to lead the simple life which they preferred. One social pleasure was entertaining a group of friends and their wives, the number never to be more than ten, for supper every two weeks. The food was always simple and the talk stimulating.

However, Franklin Roosevelt cared most about his work. Since boyhood he had been reading and studying about the Navy. His information now proved valuable. He already knew much that he would have had to learn. He saw into matters so quickly that one Rear-Admiral described him as a "man with a flashing mind." He became known as "the economizer." Another naval officer said, "He makes you feel that he wants every penny to go into the fighting strength and not into show."

31

Roosevelt's talent for getting along with people proved valuable, too. The naval officers liked him because he could make instant decisions. He could also end any argument, however hot it might be, with a laugh.

Josephus Daniels, a newspaper editor from Raleigh, North Carolina, was Secretary of the Navy and therefore Roosevelt's chief. The two men liked each other and enjoyed working together. The World War was already in progress. Secretary Daniels and Assistant-Secretary Roosevelt saw that it was only a matter of time until the United States would be drawn into that war across the Atlantic Ocean. They tried to get the Navy into its best condition in order to be ready when this country declared war. They succeeded remarkably.

In his zeal to be prepared, Roosevelt bought every kind of supply which he thought the Navy might need in a war. So thoroughly did he buy that one day he received an order to report at the White House. He found President Wilson talking to General Scott, Chief of Staff of the Army, and the man who did the buying for the Army.

"Mr. Secretary," said President Wilson to Franklin Roosevelt, smiling, "it seems you have cornered the market on supplies. I'm sorry, but you'll have to divide up with the Army."

Franklin Roosevelt found that a number of men in the Navy could not swim. As a result, some of the sailors drowned when they fell off docks or boats. Roosevelt made a rule that every man in the Navy must learn to swim. A rule was not enough; he wanted the men to feel a pride in swimming. He, therefore, gave a silver cup, known as the Assistant-Secretary's cup, for which the battleship crews tried each year. The test was a dive from a height of not less than eighteen feet followed by an unaided swim of at least a hundred yards. The cup was to be held by the ship having the largest number of swimmers, from the commanding officer down.

Personal courage was always one of Roosevelt's traits. He showed this in 1915. A submarine, the F-4, was sunk, with everybody on board, near Hawaii. Roosevelt happened to be in San Francisco when the tragedy occurred. In order to keep sailors from fearing duty on submarines, he at once went down in a submarine off the Pacific coast.

After the United States entered World War I, Roosevelt was as busy as one person could possibly be. He wanted to inspect the naval bases in European waters and on July 9th, 1918, he left on a destroyer.

The Atlantic Ocean was filled with German submarine boats which sank ships of other nations. This gave grave danger to the trip; in fact, a submarine did come perilously near the destroyer and might have sunk it but did not. Roosevelt would not worry. Hundreds of thousands of American soldiers had run the risk of crossing; why shouldn't he? Because he was Assistant-Secretary of the Navy, he could have gone on a large and comfortable vessel. He would not go that way, but insisted on going on a small destroyer where his

narrow bunk was only a little better than the bunks
of the sailors. The trip was very rough. He wrote about
it: "One has to hang on to something all the time—
never move without taking hold with one hand before
letting go with another. Much of the crockery smashed.
Three of the officers were quite ill but, so far, I am
all right."

The crossing was made in safety. Inspection trips,
both in England and France, filled his time abroad.
He met all the heads of foreign governments fighting
on the side of the Allies. For a short time naval affairs
were put aside, and he went up on the battle front.

On the return trip to the United States, made on
an enormous passenger boat, the *Leviathan,* he developed his old "catching" habit about illnesses. Influenza
was raging, and he promptly caught it. The influenza
developed into pneumonia. By the time the *Leviathan*
reached New York, Franklin Roosevelt was so ill that
he had to be taken off the *Leviathan* on a stretcher.
When he recovered, World War I was about over.

The war had done many things for him. Through
his own hard work and energy, he had become known
as efficient and able. He had met the Allied leaders
—Foch, Clemenceau, Lloyd George and the King of
England—and had seen a great deal of the actual war.
During President Wilson's administration, while Josephus Daniels and Franklin Roosevelt were in charge
of the Navy, the Navy had grown from 43,000 men to
500,000; from about 3,000 officers to 32,000; and from
326 ships to 1,000. The Navy had spent an enormous
sum—over four billion dollars—and yet a Senate com-

mittee which investigated all war expenses found no hint of scandal. Secretary Daniels and Assistant-Secretary Roosevelt were naturally proud of this achievement. They had had two big jobs: to protect America and to protect ships full of soldiers crossing the Atlantic Ocean to France. They had done both expertly.

During the Washington years, the family life of the Roosevelts was very eventful. Three sons were born to them; the parents suffered the sorrow of the death of one when he was only eight months old. There were illnesses among the children. In the summer of 1915, while his wife and children were at Campobello, Franklin himself had appendicitis without warning. And throughout all these happenings, Mrs. Roosevelt ran her home so well that it was considered a model of wartime management.

January 2nd, 1920, Franklin Roosevelt went back to Europe to wind up the Navy's affairs on the other side of the Atlantic. His wife went with him. While he traveled from place to place, Mrs. Roosevelt stayed in Paris visiting hospitals full of wounded American boys. This second trip, finished in about six weeks, increased Roosevelt's personal friendships with important men abroad. The Roosevelts returned to America on the same ship which brought President and Mrs. Woodrow Wilson back from the Peace Conference in Paris. This boat trip together helped to establish an even closer friendship between President Wilson and Franklin Roosevelt, a friendship which Roosevelt always treasured.

Roosevelt believed passionately in the League of

Nations. This strong belief was one of the ties which bound him and President Wilson together. In every speech he made during this time, Roosevelt stated that he was for the League, saying, "The League may not end wars, but the nations demand the experiment."

CHAPTER SEVEN

A RACE FOR THE VICE-PRESIDENCY

The national Democratic convention, held during the summer of 1920, chose James M. Cox, Governor of Ohio, to run for the Presidency. The convention then looked around for a strong man to run for the Vice-President's place on the ticket with Cox. Franklin Roosevelt was nominated by acclamation, and he was seconded in a stirring speech by his old friend, Governor Alfred E. Smith of New York State. Only thirty-eight years old, Mr. Roosevelt was quite young for such a place. He had been in politics less than ten years, seven of which he had served as Assistant-Secretary of the Navy.

Franklin Roosevelt began his campaign in a speech of acceptance of the nomination, made from the front piazza of his home at Hyde Park. A life-long neighbor escorted him out on the piazza before a cheering crowd of five thousand friends and neighbors.

The neighbor introduced Roosevelt by saying simply, "Here's our boy," and the crowd cheered wildly.

In his speech, Roosevelt said, "All my life I have tried to do things in the open, where anyone could see and where nothing was concealed. . . . I hope that will be the spirit of the campaign."

There was little chance of a Democratic victory, but

James M. Cox, left, Governor of Ohio, and Franklin Roosevelt,
right, leading a parade during the 1920 campaign. Cox and Roosevelt, the Democratic candidates for the Presidency and Vice-Presidency, respectively, were defeated.

Roosevelt stuck to his belief in putting up the best
fight possible. Years before, young and inexperienced,
he had fought for a place in the senate of New York
State. He now threw himself into this national campaign with that same energy. He traveled over the
United States, making thousands of speeches. Mrs.
Roosevelt went with him. She had conquered her early
shyness and she often talked to women's clubs while
he spoke to groups of men. He took many side trips
from the special train, trying to meet as many people
as possible.

In spite of the hard fight put up by Franklin Roosevelt and Cox, they were both beaten. The Republican candidates, Harding and Coolidge, won. Franklin Roosevelt suffered from this defeat in running for public office. Losing discouraged him. He had almost always been a victor before and could not understand this defeat.

After the election was over, Franklin took a needed vacation, then returned to the practice of law in New York City. There were now five children to provide for, and his salary in political life had been small. He felt that he should do what he could to build up a paying law business.

In addition to attending to business, he undertook several public matters. Helping with the Boy Scout movement in New York State was one. Taking an active interest in Harvard University, of which he had been elected an Overseer, or Trustee, was another. Becoming chairman of a committee to raise money for the Woodrow Wilson Foundation to promote peace, was a third. Thus he served as a useful citizen and also earned a living for his family.

CHAPTER EIGHT

INFANTILE PARALYSIS

The next summer, 1921, a tragedy occurred. At his summer home at Campobello Island, near the Maine coast, Franklin Roosevelt developed infantile paralysis. He had not felt well for several days beforehand and had been very tired ever since his race for the Vice-Presidency. He was thus in a condition to yield to any germ. The attack came immediately after a swim in the icy waters of the Bay of Fundy while he was overheated from a run across the island with his boys. An epidemic of the terrible disease raged in New York City, but no other case existed within miles of Campobello. Another cause for anxiety was the fear lest his children become ill from the same trouble, but fortunately none of them did.

After slight improvement, Roosevelt was moved to a hospital in New York City for treatment. A group of his friends from Eastport, Maine, just across from Campobello, went to tell him goodbye on the day he was taken away on a stretcher. These men were very depressed over his helplessness. It was told afterward, as an instance of his gallant spirit, that he lay there flat on his back and waved at his friends, smiled cheerily, and said, "I'll see you again when I am President of the United States."

When he left the hospital, his mother expected him

to return to Hyde Park and make his home there. She hoped that the quiet life and peaceful surroundings of Hyde Park would improve his health, though she never expected him to be active again. Since he could not walk, she hoped that perhaps he would write a book, the contents of which he had had in mind but had never found time to put on paper. Her son did not agree with her loving plans for a quiet life for him. He had no idea of giving up. Instead of returning to Hyde Park, he went from the hospital to his home on Sixty-fifth Street, and the days began to be much as they had been before.

His friends who first came to see him after the illness received a great surprise. They came with long faces, prepared to grieve with him because he would probably be helpless for the rest of his life. He gaily declined their sympathy and would not even talk of his sickness, as invalids generally enjoy doing. Instead, he plunged at once into eager talk with the callers about matters in which he was interested. No one heard him complain about his hard lot. He decided that he would not let a "childish" disease ruin his life. He would not let his illness be mentioned, and he insisted on being treated as a sound, well man. Above the waist-line, his health and strength were as superb as ever. His legs simply would not move unless they were moved for him. His wife helped him in every way in his iron resolution to ignore his physical handicap. Two things came with him out of the illness. They were a grim determination to walk again, and a passionate desire to help other people who had suffered from infantile paralysis. It is interesting to know how he accomplished these aims.

He began to find, strangely enough, that there were almost advantages in possessing helpless legs. He wasted neither time nor energy in moving from one place to another. He did not go to see people; everyone came to see him. Because he felt so well, he had always been a person of great physical energy. Now that he had to sit still in one spot, all his energy went into putting his mind on any subject brought to his attention. He read a great deal and continued to learn. He kept up with his two hobbies—collecting stamps and models of ships.

One of the most delightful sensations of his life came after many weary months. He was able to wiggle his toes! By the summer of 1922 the wiggling motion gave him hope that his dead legs would slowly improve because feeling and movement had returned to the toes. He learned to walk on crutches. Gradually he resumed the practice of law.

Besides his wife, one other person proved most important in his recovery. This was Louis Howe, the newspaper man who had become a friend while Roosevelt was in the New York Senate. Louis Howe had gone to Washington and helped during Roosevelt's term as Assistant-Secretary of the Navy. When Roosevelt was taken ill, Howe had come to Campobello to say goodbye before accepting a business position at a fine salary. For years Mr. Howe had loved and admired Roosevelt. He was so impressed by Roosevelt's fighting spirit in trying to get well that he declined the business position and stayed to help both Mr. and Mrs. Roosevelt in any way that he could. Howe attended business and political meetings in Mr. Roosevelt's place; he kept Mr. Roosevelt informed as to what was going on in the world. He became Mr. Roosevelt's other self.

For three years Franklin Roosevelt took exercises and tried various forms of treatment for his helpless legs. It required an iron will to keep doing the exercises when little improvement resulted; he never lost courage, though, and kept on with the exercises.

George Foster Peabody, a rich man from New York who did a great deal of good, told Roosevelt about Warm Springs, Georgia. Warm Springs was a rundown old summer resort with a wooden hotel, a few small summer cottages, and a pool of naturally warm water. A person could swim in the warm pool for hours and yet come out feeling fine. Mr. Peabody told Mr. Roosevelt the story of a young man who had been helpless from the effects of infantile paralysis, and the doctors thought he would never walk again. The first summer at Warm Springs the helpless young man found that, wearing a life preserver, he could move his legs while in the water, and he learned to swim. The second summer he stood up in the water. The third summer he could walk anywhere on land with the aid of canes.

Mr. Roosevelt already knew that exercise would be the only thing to help restore the muscles injured by infantile paralysis. He knew that it is much easier to exercise in water because the water holds a person up

Franklin Roosevelt swimming in the Warm Springs pool in its early days. Because he was benefited by swimming there, he established the Warm Springs Foundation so that other polio sufferers might be helped also.

and takes all the weight off the muscles. And the warmer the water, the easier it is to exercise. The water in the Warm Springs pool was naturally warm all the time.

Mr. Peabody's story so impressed Mr. Roosevelt that in the fall of 1924 he went to Warm Springs. A fine swimmer before his illness, he stayed for six weeks, swimming daily in the warm water of the pool. As a result of the swimming, at the end of six weeks he showed more improvement than in the previous three years.

People who had had infantile paralysis heard how Franklin Roosevelt had been helped, and they began to flock to Warm Springs. Warm Springs had no way to care for these afflicted persons, many of whom were without money. Roosevelt told a national convention of doctors how Warm Springs had helped him and others who were crippled by infantile paralysis. The convention of doctors approved the establishment of a health center at Warm Springs. Mr. Roosevelt undertook to raise the money to make Warm Springs into a useful institution. He bought the springs, the hotel, the cottages and about twelve hundred acres of land from Mr. Peabody. January 1927, he established the title of Warm Springs Foundation, a nonprofit-making institution. Through Mr. Roosevelt's efforts, and aided by his friends, those early plans have grown until Warm Springs continually assists many helpless people back to useful lives.

Since the project at Warm Springs has shown what can be done, several other places in the United States have established institutions like Warm Springs. At these, more crippled people may be treated and helped than could possibly be cared for at Warm Springs. Mr. Roosevelt wrote many articles and made numerous speeches in behalf of infantile paralysis sufferers. Through his determination to get well, numerous other patients have, as he did, made up their minds not to ask special favors of the world because they are crippled.

For eight years Mr. Roosevelt stayed out of active politics, but he remained keenly interested in all public matters, and his opinion carried great influence in national affairs. During the famous Democratic convention of 1924, which was held in New York City, he nominated Al Smith for the Presidency. He stood on crutches while he made the speech, in which he called Al Smith the "Happy Warrior." In spite of not being able to walk without help, he looked healthy and happy.

The *Evening World* wrote of him: "No matter whether Governor Smith wins or loses, Franklin Roosevelt stands out as the real hero of the Democratic convention of 1924. . . . Roosevelt might be a pathetic figure but for the fine courage that flashes in his smile."

When his friends wanted him to run for public office, he always answered, "Wait until I get rid of crutches." Several years passed. It looked as if he might be able to walk without crutches; yet he still refused to think about public office. Staying out of politics increased his influence. The Democratic leaders paid attention to his opinion because he did not want any-

During the famous Democratic Convention of 1924, Franklin Roosevelt, on crutches, nominated Al Smith, extreme right, for the Presidency, in a speech in which he called Al Smith the "Happy Warrior." Said newspapers of that occasion, "Franklin Roosevelt stands out as the real hero. He (Roosevelt) might be a pathetic figure but for the fine courage that flashes in his smile."

thing for himself but thought only of the good of the Democratic party. His reputation was made. He did not have to do anything more to increase it.

Warm Springs became his second home. He bought a farm there. Living in Georgia for several months each year enabled him to know Southern people, and he made many true friends in the South. In fact, he had friends in every state in the Union; he kept in touch with them through letters.

Mrs. Roosevelt had also become active politically. Beginning with the tour of the United States when her husband had run for the Vice-Presidency in 1920, she helped the women's section of the national Democratic party.

CHAPTER NINE

DRAFTED FOR GOVERNOR

October 1928 arrived. Al Smith's fourth term as Governor of the State of New York neared its end. He was running for the Presidency of the United States on the Democratic ticket. The New York State Democratic convention met in Albany to find someone to succeed Al Smith as Governor. Mr. Roosevelt had gone to Warm Springs. Before he left, the state leaders wanted Mr. Roosevelt to agree to run for governor, but he steadily refused, even though he no longer had to use crutches; he walked with a cane and the support of someone's arm.

Al Smith felt that his own chances for winning the Presidency would be stronger if Mr. Roosevelt were Governor of New York, because New York sends such a large number of delegates to the national Democratic convention. Smith urged Roosevelt to accept the nomination for Governor, but Roosevelt still declined. There was no doubt about his being well enough to do the work as Governor. His general health was excellent. He simply did not want the job, though Al Smith and other friends continued to beg him to take it. He hated to decline in the face of Al Smith's plea. He remembered with gratitude Al Smith's kindness and good advice to him when he was a young senator at Albany.

On the morning of October 1st, Roosevelt sent Smith a telegram from Warm Springs. It read:

"I wish very much that I might even consider the possibility of running for Governor this year, especially if by doing so I could further help you, but there are two considerations which are compelling. First, your own record in New York State is so clear to the voters that you will carry the state regardless of who is nominated for Governor and my nomination would make no difference to your success on the New York ticket. Secondly, my doctors are very specific in stating that the continued improvement in my condition is dependent on my avoidance of cold climate and on taking exercises here at Warm Springs during the cold winter months. It probably means getting rid of leg braces during the next two winters, and that would be impossible if I had to remain at Albany. As I am only forty-six years of age, I feel that I owe it to my family and myself to give the present constant improvement a chance to continue. I must therefore with great regret confirm my decision not to accept the nomination, and I know you will understand.—FRANKLIN D. ROOSEVELT."

After the telegram had gone, Mr. Roosevelt felt afraid that Smith would beg him to change his mind. Mr. Roosevelt therefore planned to stay away from a phone all day in order that Smith could not talk to him. Sure enough, Smith did try to call him. Smith could not get him during the morning because Mr. Roosevelt was swimming in the pool. After the swim, Mr. Roosevelt went off on a picnic—on purpose. After the picnic, he attended a night meeting at a near-by town—also on purpose. All those hours Smith kept steadily calling Mr. Roosevelt over the phone. Of course Smith could not get him.

During the night meeting a messenger pushed near the speaker's platform and said that the New York wire was being held at a drug store until Mr. Roosevelt could come to the phone. Mr. Roosevelt, who was talking, only spoke that much longer. When finally he did go to the phone, he could not hear because the connection was bad. After his return to Warm Springs, late that night, answering the phone could not be put off any longer. He was obliged to talk to the Democratic leaders at Albany. They pleaded with him to accept the nomination for governor. He steadily declined. Al Smith then begged him not to say "No" if he were nominated.

The matter was left that way. Mr. Roosevelt would not say "Yes," and yet he did not say a final "No." The men at Albany were joyful. They believed that he would accept if nominated. Next morning the Albany convention drafted him, and he was enthusiastically chosen as the Democratic candidate for Governor of New York State.

This joy was not shared by all Mr. Roosevelt's friends and family. Some of those who were closest to him feared that his recovery would be delayed and his general health endangered by his return to public life. They felt that he might even be endangering his life by agreeing to help a friend.

They were so gloomy over the prospect that finally

Mr. Roosevelt said cheerfully, "Well, if I've got to run for Governor, there's no use in all of us getting sick over it."

These people later were to find themselves mistaken about the bad effect on his health, but they did not know it at that time, so they continued to worry about him.

Mr. Roosevelt had always believed in making the best fight possible about anything, whether large or small. He had not wanted to run for the governorship; once the matter was settled, and he had accepted the nomination, he threw himself into the fight with every bit of his tireless energy. He traveled up and down the big state of New York. He made numerous public speeches, telling the people exactly for what he stood. To the people whom he could not meet face to face, he talked over the radio. He fought as hard a battle as he had eighteen years before when, as a young man, he had run for the state senate.

The sight of him well and strong, except for his inability to walk without a cane and the help of someone's arm, set at rest many rumors that he could not stand the strain of the governorship. Best of all, he thrived on the excitement and the constant traveling. He enjoyed every minute of it.

He said, "If I could campaign another six months, I believe I could throw away my cane."

The newspapers stood behind him. Even those papers which opposed him declared in print that he would, if elected, be able to perform his duties as well physically as any war veteran who had lost an arm or a leg in battle.

Judged by their heavy votes, the people of New York State must have decided that it was more important to have a Governor with a good brain than one with good legs. On November 9th, 1928, the citizens of New York State, by a large vote, elected Franklin Delano Roosevelt their Governor. The election was a tribute to Mr. Roosevelt's ability, his sense of justice, his friendliness to everybody, and his charm of manner. The fact that he had risen above political parties appealed alike to Democrats and Republicans.

While Mr. Roosevelt won his race, Al Smith lost his race for the Presidency. That fact lessened Mr. Roosevelt's pleasure in his own victory. He had run for the governorship largely to help Smith become President. Al Smith's defeat disappointed him more than if he himself had lost.

Hyde Park naturally celebrated the election of its "boy" to the highest office in the state. Hadn't he been born at Hyde Park, ridden a pony along the country roads, sailed up and down the Hudson River, represented Dutchess County in the state senate? Hyde Park was immensely proud of "our Governor."

But Warm Springs, Mr. Roosevelt's second home, went wild with delight. The only regret was that Mr. Roosevelt could not go down to Warm Springs to join in the celebration over his election.

Again the Roosevelt family prepared to move to Albany. Eighteen years before, they had occupied a rented house in Albany while Franklin Roosevelt served as senator. This time they would live in the roomy Executive Mansion which the Governor of New York occupies. And there was no doubt but that Mrs. Roosevelt would make a real home of it, as she had made of every house in which they had lived. In order that swimming at Warm Springs might not be missed, a greenhouse at the Mansion was made into a swimming pool.

The first thing the Governor-elect ordered was that less money be spent on his inauguration. Mr. Roosevelt believed in economy, both in personal and in public matters. He came of Dutch people who did not waste money even when there was plenty of it.

On New Year's Day, 1929, in a very simple ceremony, he became Governor of the State of New York. While he took the oath of office in the State Capitol, his hand rested on a Bible which had been in his family for two hundred years. It came down from Jacobus Roosevelt, a grandson of Claes Roosevelt, who founded the Roosevelt family in America, back in 1644. And on the platform that day was Mrs. Sarah Delano Roosevelt, a mother very proud of her son.

That New Year's Day was very important to Franklin Roosevelt. It marked his return from sickness and invalidism to public life. The event convinced him and everyone else that his health was well-nigh perfect. If this had not been the case, how could he have improved under the strain of a hard campaign? He now drove a car and rode horseback. He walked and swam as well.

He returned to public life, a finer and more able

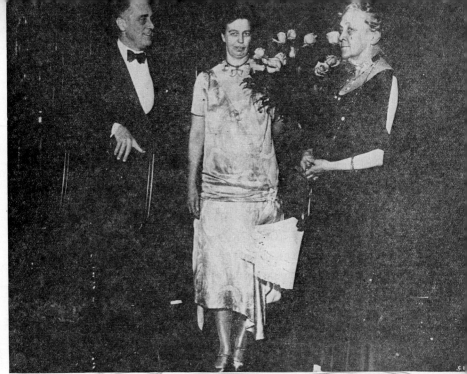
Mr. Roosevelt, his wife and mother at reception following his
inauguration as Governor of New York State.

person than before his illness. When the paralysis set
in he was a gay, good-humored, handsome young man
to whom the good things of life had been given in
full measure. His desperate fight to get well had matured him, made him see the serious side of life. It had
also developed in him self-discipline and iron will-
power. He had had time to study and to think. His face
showed lines of pain and suffering; it also showed
more strength and a new understanding. In fact, he
seemed a different person from the man who had been
taken ill at Campobello Island in the summer of 1921.

CHAPTER TEN

ACHIEVEMENTS OF THE GOVERNOR

That New Year's Day not only began his term as Governor of a rich and important state; it became the first step along the road which later led to the White House. A man who can manage the State of New York with success receives excellent training for the Presidency, and many governors of New York have gone on to the Presidency. Perhaps Franklin Roosevelt did not then think that he might later become President. If he did, he gave no sign.

There was plenty of work for Governor Roosevelt to do and he plunged into it at once. He continued the reforms begun by Al Smith and started some of his own. He had always fought for reforms since, as editor of the Harvard *Crimson,* he had won his fight to have Harvard's dormitories equipped with fire escapes. His plans as governor included relief for the unemployed, help for the farmers, planting more trees through reforestation, public development of water power, old age pensions, and getting people to leave the crowded cities in order to live on farms.

He soon showed that he meant to be an independent governor. Problems arose from the fact that he was a Democratic governor and the Legislature was largely Republican. This state of affairs led to clashes between the two parties and with the Governor.

When the two parties tried to boss him, he declared, "I wasn't anxious to be Governor but now that I am, I beg to remind you that I *am* Governor."

Governor Roosevelt had to take one public matter to the court for settlement. The lower courts decided against him, but he carried the battle on to the higher Court of Appeals and that court decided for him. This decision in his favor by the Court of Appeals helped him in future dealings with the Legislature.

Whenever he fought with any group, he thoroughly enjoyed the battle. He had said, when a young senator, "There's nothing I love as much as a good fight," and he showed that trait again and again. But he never lost his temper during any fight.

The duties of the office of Governor were heavy, but Mr. Roosevelt took time to speak and write on public matters, both those in New York State and in the United States. Someone called him "nationally-minded."

Governor Roosevelt wanted to see conditions and talk to people himself. He believed that he could not govern intelligently until he had been in every county and had become acquainted with the problems of all the citizens.

The summer after he took office he traveled over the State, visiting towns, villages and crossroads which had not seen a governor for years. Because he had been reared on the farm at Hyde Park, he knew about farm matters and could talk farm problems. In fact, the farmers said he was the first farmer-governor in many years. He traveled by car over the highways and by barges along the state system of canals. These trips were more like picnics than work to him and were a great rest from the problems which he had to settle in Albany. The second summer he took more and more trips, until he had covered the state. During his first term he probably traveled more miles, and made more speeches, than any other governor had done in the same length of time.

He was not solely a traveling governor, however. He did a great amount of hard work at his desk. The end of a long day in the office would find everyone worn out but him. He remained quite fresh and in the best of spirits, ready to joke and laugh with late callers.

Mrs. Roosevelt had a share in making her husband a successful governor. She had become deeply interested in public matters and was in touch with every important activity. Her interest in politics started with her desire to bring political news to her husband while he was recovering from infantile paralysis. Louis Howe was her teacher. When she began to make her first public speeches in 1921, Mr. Howe sat in the back of the hall and listened to her. Afterward he told her what to say and what to leave out. One bit of advice was—"Say what you have to say and sit down."

While serving as the First Lady at Albany, she still found time to keep up her own interests. She continued to teach in the Todhunter School in New York City for the first two and a half days each week. Every Sunday night she took the train to New York where she taught Monday, Tuesday, and a part of Wednesday. Wednesday she took a train back to Albany, arriving for the weekly public reception or "At Home." The rest of the week she devoted to being an official hostess, to writing magazine articles and making speeches, to running several homes, and to looking after her family. She drove her own car and rode horseback when she could find time. She was also a partner in a small furniture factory started at Hyde Park in order to provide work for the village people and to make good copies of early American furniture.

Governor Roosevelt stood the strain of his office so well that he decided to run for another term as governor. During the second campaign, he made from one to fourteen speeches a day.

The day of the fourteenth speech was cold and rainy; most of the time he spoke standing up in an open car in the rain. He seldom mentioned his physical infirmity but that night he did.

When he arose to make the last speech he said, "This is my fourteenth appearance today. Not bad for the helpless, hopeless invalid that the Republican party talked about two years ago." Of course, the audience cheered loudly.

An evidence of his fine health occurred in the midst of this campaign. He stood an examination for life insurance. To secure life insurance, a person has to be in excellent physical condition. If he is not altogether well, he may obtain the insurance, but he will be required to pay a higher rate because of the risk involved in his uncertain health.

In October, 1930, Governor Roosevelt obtained five hundred thousand dollars' worth of life insurance at the normal rate for a man of his age. Not a dollar of extra premium was charged because his legs would not move without assistance. The insurance was for the Georgia Warm Springs Foundation in order to help that institution take care of crippled patients if anything happened to him.

The doctor who made the medical examination said to Governor Roosevelt, "I wish to congratulate you on obtaining $500,000 worth of life insurance. I also wish to say that it has rarely been my privilege as an examining physician for life insurance to see such a splendid physical specimen as yourself."

One reason for Governor Roosevelt's good health was that he never worried. His strong sense of humor was another reason. He laughed a great deal, and a good laugh is a wonderful tonic. A newspaper man said that Franklin Roosevelt probably laughed more times a day than anyone in politics. Perhaps the real reason behind the laughter lay in the fact that he generally enjoyed politics as well as life. Anyway, when he finished the second campaign, he looked as fresh as when he started.

The patients at Warm Springs followed with keen interest his fight for the second term. They raised $150, a very large sum for them, and sent it as their gift to the campaign expenses. The gift touched Governor Roosevelt very much.

He was re-elected by the greatest vote ever cast for a governor in the history of New York. Immediately afterward, he left for a real vacation at Warm Springs, where he received the sincerest of welcomes.

At Warm Springs he lived in the little white cottage which he had built and entered heartily into the life of the place. Each morning he took regular exercises in the glass-enclosed pool. Afterward he played water games with the children in the pool, a sport which gave them keen delight. Each afternoon he rode over the near-by farm he had bought, enjoying the outdoor warmth and sunshine.

He also enjoyed watching the growth of Warm Springs from a place with no accommodations for cripples to an institution which, in 1930, treated 248 sufferers from infantile paralysis. The patients, from babies to old folks, were cheerful and lively instead of low-spirited and gloomy. This courage and cheerfulness was largely inspired by Franklin Roosevelt who, from the very beginning of his illness, had shown such a fine spirit himself. He had not whined because he was crippled; no one at Warm Springs whined either. He always left Warm Springs refreshed in mind and body. The love of the patients helped his mind; the swimming in warm water helped his legs.

He returned to Albany looking and feeling fine.

CHAPTER ELEVEN

NOMINATION FOR THE PRESIDENCY

The newspapers and people began immediately to talk about him as the next President of the United States. Some friends asked his wife if he was well enough to stand the physical strain of that high office.

She answered, "If infantile paralysis couldn't kill him, the Presidency certainly couldn't!"

The Democrats in North Dakota asked Governor Roosevelt's permission to print his name on the tickets for the approaching primary election in their state. His letter of reply was very frank and honest.

He wrote: "I willingly give my consent. It is the simple duty of every American to serve if called upon . . . However, our legislature is now in session and I must devote myself to the obtaining of progressive laws. Were I now to divert my efforts in furtherance of my own political future, I would stamp myself as one unworthy of my party's choice as leader."

Governor Roosevelt's decision to run disappointed Al Smith because he still hoped to be President. Al counted on his friend Franklin Roosevelt to nominate him again at the coming Democratic convention, which Roosevelt had done three times before (1920, 1924, 1928). Some leaders of the Democratic party, however, felt that Al Smith could not win as he had had two opportunities and had lost each time. The Democratic leaders were anxious to nominate a new person who really stood a chance of winning.

It was a very important occasion. For several years the United States had been in the grip of a depression. Many people were jobless and hungry; many others were discouraged and desperate. There was need to choose a wise and able leader.

During the months before the election, Governor Roosevelt often said that if he were elected President, he hoped to give the people a square deal. The newspapers changed his words a bit; "square deal" became "New Deal" and thus this designation has remained ever since.

The last of June 1932, the Democratic National Convention met at Chicago and nominated Franklin D. Roosevelt as its candidate for the Presidency. It had always been the custom to notify a man of his nomination several weeks after the convention was over. Mr. Roosevelt thought this a useless custom. He listened over the radio to the convention proceedings in Chicago.

Very soon after the deciding ballot was cast, he sent this telegram to the convention:

"I thank you. It is customary to hold formal notification ceremonies several weeks after the convention. This involves great expense. Instead, may I ask the convention to remain in session tomorrow so that I may appear before you and be notified at that time?

—F. D. Roosevelt."

The crowd at Chicago promptly agreed to stay until he arrived.

He broke one custom by asking to be notified at once and thus save the expense of another gathering a little later. He broke another custom by flying to Chicago from Albany on July 3. With him went Mrs. Roosevelt and the two younger sons who had not gone to the convention. His plane took only a few hours to make the trip. Thousands of people welcomed him at the Chicago airport and thousands more at the huge Stadium where the convention was held. When he walked slowly up the Stadium aisle, the delegates stood on chairs and shouted and cheered him. After the crowd had at last grown quiet, he was formally notified and accepted. His speech of acceptance ended with this challenge:

"I pledge myself to a New Deal for the American people. This is more than a political campaign. It is a call to arms!"

The huge crowd took it as a call to arms. They cheered again and again. The delegates returned to their homes determined to elect Franklin Roosevelt.

Mr. Roosevelt entered the race with one great advantage in his favor, besides his ability. For a number of years he had carried on a large correspondence with numbers of people all over the United States. He had always answered every single letter that had come to him. He did not send a form letter as a reply but wrote a personal, special letter. He had thus made many devoted friends who were not only willing but extremely anxious to do anything possible to make him President.

Two weeks before the Democratic Convention, the Republicans had nominated Herbert Hoover, who had already served one term as President. Years before, while Roosevelt lived in Washington as Assistant-Secretary of the Navy, the Franklin Roosevelts and the Herbert Hoovers had become good friends. Now the two former friends were both running for the highest office in the land.

After his return from Chicago, Roosevelt went for a little cruise along the New England coast. He and three of his sons manned the boat and did all the work, even the cooking.

This vacation on the salt water he loved was a preparation for a hard-fought campaign which took him across the continent and back again. Altogether the special train traveled seventeen-thousand miles. During the trip Roosevelt showed the same remarkable strength he had when running for Governor; everyone else was exhausted while he remained quite untired. He declined to have a doctor on the campaign train though men running for the Presidency usually took a physician along; nor did he have need for a doctor.

At times he left the train and drove in an open car from which he spoke. One hot day he addressed a meeting in Kansas. It was so hot that the newspaper men, who wore hats, could not endure the intense heat but had to get in the shade. Mr. Roosevelt, bareheaded, stood in the blazing sun for over an hour and was none the worse for it. The entire trip by car through New England was made in a cold rain; he did not even catch a cold.

He also made many radio speeches. Someone has said that "his voice, like his eyes, always carries a smile." This magnificent voice enabled him to talk very successfully over the radio. He used short, easy words because he believed that every citizen should be able to understand the government.

Early November ended the exciting campaign. Both Democrats and Republicans were sure of the victory in advance. However, the election returns showed that the Democrats had won and that Franklin Delano Roosevelt would be the next President of the United States. He had received the greatest number of votes ever cast for a President and had defeated Mr. Hoover. Many people and states which usually voted the Republican ticket had changed to the Democratic side because they believed in the things for which Mr. Roosevelt and the "New Deal" stood.

CHAPTER TWELVE

PREPARING FOR THE PRESIDENCY

The week after the election, Mr. Roosevelt went to Warm Springs to rest and swim. The stay could not last very long. He was still Governor of New York State and had to hurry back to that job. On January 1st a new governor came into office, which left Mr. Roosevelt a private citizen until March 4th. There was not much rest nor privacy. He must consider who would be the members of his new Cabinet. He had to talk to many important people about national matters. It was necessary to work long hours every day in order to see all these people and get their opinions. Fortunately, the amount of work he could do was always a marvel to his helpers. The harder the work, the more he seemed to thrive on it. At that time, he worked from early morning until late at night, sixteen and eighteen hours a day, without getting tired.

He went to Warm Springs to celebrate his fifty-first birthday on January 30th and he cut a huge birthday cake with fifty-one candles. He blew out the candles himself while the patients at the birthday dinner cheered wildly, for both doctors and patients adored him.

Though a terrific worker, he knew the value of play. Perhaps he remembered the old saying that "all work and no play makes Jack a dull boy." He took time to

go South on a two weeks' fishing trip off the coast of
Florida. Since his boyhood days, when he had wanted
to attend Annapolis, he had loved the sea, the sight of
the tossing waves and the smell of salt in the air. A
vacation on a boat was always a great joy. This boat
was an elegant yacht belonging to Vincent Astor, a
close friend, and a very different vessel from the old
sailboat on which he and his sons had cruised the previous summer. The small group on the yacht were old
friends and relatives; the trip was intended to be a
complete vacation from office seekers and national
problems. The fishing turned out to be excellent, and
Mr. Roosevelt was the life of the party. He played
jokes constantly on everybody.

At the end of the trip the yacht landed at Miami,
Florida, where Mr. Roosevelt would take the train back
to Washington. In order to welcome the next President, an immense crowd filled Bay Front Park. The
waters of Biscayne Bay, edging the park, washed softly
against the sea wall. Tall palm trees waved rustling
green fronds above the multitude of people. Brilliant
lights turned night into day. It was a gala occasion for
Miami.

Mr. Roosevelt stood up in an open car and made a
speech. He sat down on the back seat. A sound, as of
firecrackers popping, filled the warm air. In reality,
the sound was made by a pistol being fired. A half-
crazed man had tried to shoot Mr. Roosevelt. The bullet mercifully missed him but hit, instead, Mayor Cermack of Chicago, who was standing near Mr. Roosevelt's car. A man and a woman were also hit.

Instantly the park was filled with confusion and shouting. To rescue Mr. Roosevelt from danger, the chauffeur at once started the car which held him. Mr. Roosevelt showed the same personal courage which he had exhibited several previous times in his life. He did not think of the danger to himself but only of wounded Mayor Cermack.

"Stop this car!" Mr. Roosevelt ordered.

He had Mayor Cermack lifted into the seat beside him. He held Mayor Cermack all the way to the hospital; he said afterward that the trip seemed thirty miles long because he feared Mayor Cermack would die before the hospital was reached. All the way he kept talking to Mayor Cermack and encouraging him. At the hospital the Mayor was rushed to the operating room for an examination; he lived for several weeks, but died later as a result of the shot. The other two people who were shot recovered. The man who did the shooting could give no reason for his crime; he simply said he hated all "rulers."

After leaving the hospital, Mr. Roosevelt returned to the yacht. The members of his party on the yacht were so upset over Mr. Roosevelt's narrow escape from death that none of them could sleep. Mr. Roosevelt went to bed and slept like a log. The Secret Service man who was on guard outside Mr. Roosevelt's door said he tiptoed into the room several times during the night to make certain that the President-elect was all right. Each time he found Mr. Roosevelt sound asleep. It is extraordinary to be able to relax after such danger, but Mr. Roosevelt never worried. He simply would not worry even when others around him were sick with worry.

Several weeks passed between the return from Miami and the inauguration. Busy weeks they were to the President-elect, filled with plans and conferences with his advisers; weeks filled with great uneasiness throughout the United States. Because of runs caused by uneasy depositors, numerous banks were closing. To prevent more runs on other banks, several states and a few cities had declared bank holidays. This was a purely temporary act and did not solve the acute banking situation. Because he was going out of office so soon, President Hoover declined to take drastic action. Until he was actually President, Mr. Roosevelt declined to take action. Mr. Roosevelt had his plans all made but, like a wise general, he would not tell them beforehand. He was waiting until he had authority to carry out his plans.

A feeling of helplessness was in the air. People did not know what to do or where to turn. Everybody waited hopefully for Mr. Roosevelt to take office. The people craved a real leader in the White House. They believed that Mr. Roosevelt would prove to be that leader. Many folks felt that, overnight, he would make the banks safe and change the depression. Of course, only a maker of miracles could have done that, but it showed the vast faith of the people in Franklin D. Roosevelt.

In spite of the bank panic and worry about money, enormous crowds filled Washington for the inauguration. People came from north, east, south and west.

There were city visitors, cowboys from the prairies, Indians from the West, plain folk from the country, and many job seekers. Hundreds of flags and miles of bunting, all red, white and blue, gave the city a gay, festive air.

CHAPTER THIRTEEN

PRESIDENT FRANKLIN DELANO ROOSEVELT

The important day, March 4th, dawned cloudy and cold. The inauguration was set for noon. Long before that hour came something not on the day's program. The President-elect, with the members of his future Cabinet and their families attended a special morning service at St. John's Episcopal Church. St. John's stands directly across Lafayette Square from the White House and is known as the Church of the Presidents because, since the time of James Monroe, a pew in St. John's has been reserved for the Presidents. All the Presidents have gone to St. John's on special occasions, and those Presidents who were members of the Episcopal church have attended it regularly. St. John's has never held a more serious group than the one on that March morning. The rector prayed that the Lord would give strength to these men and the one woman Cabinet member for the heavy tasks which lay ahead.

It is the custom for the President whose term of office is out, and the incoming President, to drive together from the White House to the Capitol for the inauguration. President Hoover and President-elect Roosevelt drove in an open car down the mile length of wide Pennsylvania Avenue. Thousands of people, with serious faces, watched them along the route; many of the people had been in their places all the night before.

The air was filled with the music of military bands and the hum of countless voices.

The Vice-President is always sworn in before the President. This is done because in case of the sudden death of the President-elect the Vice-President would at once become President. The ceremony takes place in the Senate Chamber inside the Capitol.

Mr. Roosevelt watched John Nance Garner of Texas, known as Cactus Jack to his friends, take the oath of office as Vice-President. That over, the crowd poured outside, joining more people already there, until the vast space before the Capitol was packed with a hundred thousand people who sat and stood in the biting wind. Of course the seats of honor held Mrs. Franklin Roosevelt, as well as Mrs. Sarah Delano Roosevelt and all the Roosevelt family. There were, besides, many important people present who had helped elect Mr. Roosevelt.

All the two hundred thousand eyes were fixed on a runway leading to the stand in front of the Capitol. At last the President-elect appeared coming down the runway. He walked slowly, leaning on the arm of his tall eldest son, James. The Marine Band played "Hail to the Chief." And the immense crowd cheered wildly. The cheers were full of confidence that, if it could be done, the man before them would conquer the depression.

At one o'clock, Franklin Delano Roosevelt became the thirty-second President of the United States. Chief Justice Hughes, in a long black robe and black silk skull cap, administered the solemn oath. The Bible was the same huge one, inherited in the Roosevelt family, which had been used when Roosevelt became Governor of New York. While he swore to protect and defend the Constitution, the President placed his hand on one of the best known passages of the Bible in the thirteenth chapter of First Corinthians. His face was grim and set with purpose, as if he saw the burdens ahead. Just as he finished repeating the oath, the sun peeped from behind the clouds and a ray of bright sunshine fell across him like a happy sign for the future.

His inaugural speech, easy and simple to understand, made with his head thrown back and his broad shoulders squared, was a fighting speech. Courage ran through it and, as always, Americans admired a man who was not afraid. He spoke like a general leading an army to battle against the depression.

"The only thing we have to fear is fear itself," he said.

That fighting speech heartened the nation. President Roosevelt's fearlessness gave fresh courage to the people who listened. They left the inauguration with new confidence that they had a leader worthy to follow. It has been said that no President ever took office amid so much faith and trust by the people.

The address finished, the President turned to leave. The crowd cheered again and again. At the sound of the cheering, the grim look left his face. His usual ready smile flashed forth. Those cheers seemed to promise that America would follow him into new ways of doing old things.

After lunch, President Roosevelt watched the parade

of 18,000 people file past the White House reviewing stand. General Douglas MacArthur, then Chief of Staff, stood by him during the review. Then the President got down to business—and there was plenty of business waiting. At half past six o'clock Saturday evening at the White House, the ten members of the Cabinet were sworn into office by Associate Justice Cardozo of the Supreme Court. Several customs were broken on that occasion. Never before had the Cabinet been sworn in on the same day as the President. Never before had the ceremony taken place at the White House. And never before had the Cabinet included a woman, Frances Perkins, Secretary of Labor.

From six-thirty until late Saturday night, the new Cabinet members labored with President Roosevelt over what to do about the closed banks. Sunday night at eleven o'clock, the President issued a proclamation which closed every bank in the United States for four days. The banks must remain closed while plans were worked out for their reopening with safety. The President also called Congress to meet in special session the next Thursday, March 9th. On Sunday night he talked to the country by radio, that being the first of his famous "fireside chats."

The days between Monday and Thursday were crowded with work for the President and his advisers. Those days were probably the most critical time since the Civil War. The President needed all his laughter and good spirits and confidence. While his helpers were frantic over the many problems to be solved, he remained calm and serene. He saw his way ahead but others did not; they saw only gloom and financial failure. Business could not go on without the banks. It was necessary to reopen them as soon as possible. How could this best be done?

When it met on March 9th, Congress, at the President's request, promptly passed a new banking act, or law. This act allowed sound banks to reopen and required all gold money to be deposited in them. People were soon hurrying to the banks. They were busily putting back in the banks the money which fear had caused them to draw out only a little while before. The banking panic had resulted from fear; the banks were reopened through new faith.

The banking situation settled, the President turned his attention to the desperate condition of human beings. His love of people made him see their great need. Millions of workers were without jobs. Lack of jobs meant lack of food. Homes and farms were being lost because their owners had no money with which to pay taxes and interest on mortgages. The President began to fight to change these serious conditions. He fought as hard as if he were a general leading an army to war. This really was the case. The United States was in the midst of a terrible depression, and he fought to overcome it.

He fought against unemployment, poverty, ill health, child labor, low prices, long hours, poor housing conditions and other kindred problems.

Under the President's leadership, the Congress appropriated vast sums of money with which to give jobs to people. The money was to be spent in two ways:

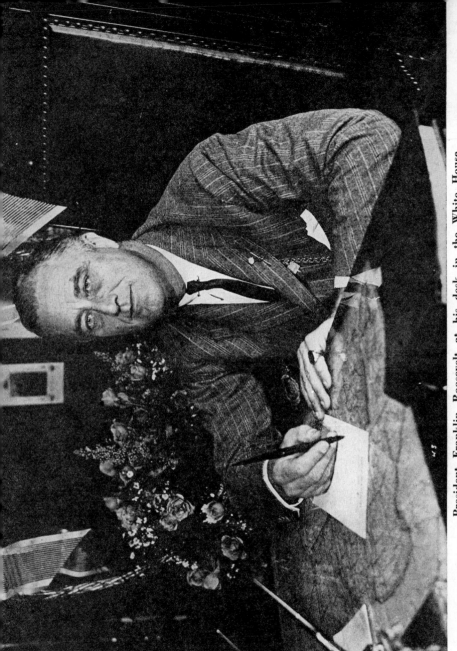

President Franklin Roosevelt at his desk in the White House.

work relief and direct relief. The President felt that people who were well and able wanted work rather than relief. It was hard to find jobs suddenly for millions of unemployed men and women. Several new government agencies, which had so many letters in their names that they were called "alphabet" agencies, started people back to work. There had to be many kinds of jobs to fit many different sorts of people. Most of the work was building. Roads, schools, parks, swimming pools, large groups of houses, were all built.

Human beings were made over, too. Jobless teachers taught men and women to read and write; women learned to sew; nurses cared for the sick; librarians brought books to those who had never had a chance to read; and farmers were taught better farming methods.

Young folk were not forgotten. The Civilian Conservation Camps (CCC) looked after men and boys out of school. The National Youth Administration (NYA) helped high school and college students.

For this work people received pay. The pay enabled them to buy things made by the farms and factories, and this meant that the farms and factories could sell their products. After four years of depression the wheels of business began to turn again. People looked and became more cheerful. A broad smile of content spread across the United States, a smile which came from the satisfaction people had in working and earning. Jobs and food formed the wide difference between hope and despair.

The President took time to attend a conference of

South American countries and the United States held in Buenos Aires, Argentina. He told the delegates to the conference that the United States wanted to be a good neighbor to the countries of South America.

According to him, a good neighbor was one who felt responsible for the welfare of those around him. This belief was shown in the President's anxiety to awaken every person to the condition of those less fortunate.

Mr. Roosevelt's first term brought several important personal changes. The White House ceased to be a cold, remote mansion and became a real home, a place full of life and gaiety and laughter. And the President laughed more often than any other member of his family. If someone wanted to find him and did not know in what room to look, the President could generally be located by the sound of his hearty laughter. Because the White House was their temporary home, the Roosevelts did not put on any airs. They continued to live as simply as they always had. But they were just as fond of company. They had a great many guests, both invited and unexpected. There was always room for another person at the table and the cook never knew how many would eat a meal she prepared. The five grown-up children and their friends came and went. The grandchildren were frequent visitors.

Another change was the death of Louis McHenry Howe in April, 1936. For months before Mr. Howe lay ill, first at the White House and later at the Naval Hospital. Even in his weakness, he knew about every political move that was made and advised the President what to do. Both President and Mrs. Roosevelt sor-

rowed over his death. For twenty-five years he had
been closely associated with them as a loyal friend,
often living in their home as a member of the family.
Mr. Howe's funeral services were held in the East
Room of the White House. The President and Mrs.
Roosevelt went with the body on a special train to
Fall River, Massachusetts, where he was buried. On
election night in 1932, Mr. Roosevelt gave a large share
of the credit for his success to Louis Howe, the shy
little newspaper man who, by his own desire, always
remained in the background and whose ambition was
realized when Franklin Roosevelt became President.

Other changes occurring were political. At first Democrats and Republicans united in helping to lift the
depression through the New Deal. Later the two parties differed. However, it appeared that the people as
a whole had faith in the New Deal and the man behind
it. The number of those who differed could not have
been very great because Franklin Roosevelt was re-
elected President for a second term in November 1936,
with only two states against him.

By an act of Congress, the date of the inauguration
had been shifted from early March to late January.
Mr. Roosevelt was the first president to be affected by
this change. On the day of his second inauguration,
the pouring rain was so cold that it almost turned to
snow. Because of the severe weather, his advisers urged
that the ceremony take place inside the Capitol. The
President would not agree. He felt that many people
had traveled long distances in order to see the event,
and if the ceremony were held indoors, the thousands

who jammed the Square before the Capitol would be cheated out of the opportunity. In spite of the cold, all of his family were on the stand, from his eighty-two year old mother to his granddaughter of two and a half years.

Justice Hughes again administered the oath of office, the wind blowing his black skull cap and white beard. President Roosevelt delivered his address with the rain beating in his face. One of the fine things he said was: "I am determined to make every American citizen the subject of his country's interest and concern." He further said: "I see a great nation, upon a great continent, blessed with great wealth of natural resources. Its hundred and thirty million people are at peace among themselves; they are making their country a good neighbor among the nations.

"In this nation I see millions of its citizens who are . . . denied . . . the necessities of life.

"I see millions of families trying to live on incomes so meager that the pall of family disaster hangs over them day by day . . .

"I see one-third of a nation ill-housed, ill-clad, ill-nourished."

He finished: "It is not in despair I paint you that picture. I paint it for you in hope, because the nation, seeing and understanding the injustice in it, purposes to paint it out."

Mrs. Roosevelt did not ride down Pennsylvania Avenue to the inauguration with the President. She joined him for the return trip. Although all the other official cars were closed, the President ordered the top of his car turned down. He said, "If the people can take the rain, I can."

Both he and Mrs. Roosevelt were as wet as the crowds they passed on the streets. Rivulets of water trickled down off the new blue hat Mrs. Roosevelt wore. The President's silk hat, which he waved often, and his clothing, were soaked. In spite of the rain, the President and Mrs. Roosevelt seemed to enjoy themselves. They smiled and waved to the people under umbrellas along the way.

A great difference was evident in the spirit of the first and second inauguration. The first one found people in the depths of despair through lack of jobs and closed banks. The second inauguration found the banks in good condition, people cheerful and most of them with jobs.

CHAPTER FOURTEEN

PREPAREDNESS

The President's first term had been filled with efforts to improve conditions in the United States. His second term continued that work, but another problem soon appeared. It was to try to keep the United States out of the World War toward which the nations seemed to be heading. Though the warlike situation was in Europe, yet its dark shadow fell across the wide Atlantic Ocean and upon the peace-loving Americas. As an early effort toward staying out of war, in January 1937, Congress passed an arms embargo act that prevented direct or indirect shipping of arms to Spain or other countries at war. The United States thus hoped to remain neutral in the approaching struggle.

The United States had always disliked dictatorships or rule by force; dictatorships destroyed the spirit of liberty and government by the people on which this country was founded. This dislike increased with Germany's rising persecution of the small, democratic countries of Europe. These countries had been seeking to give the common man a better chance and a fuller life, and the United States approved of this principle. The United States therefore showed its disapproval of Germany's methods by calling home the American Ambassador to Germany as a protest. He came first for a short stay and later was ordered to remain.

The safety of the United States depends on that of Canada and South America; it would be difficult, if not impossible for the United States to remain at peace if these adjoining countries should become involved in war. The President therefore desired to continue this Good Neighbor policy with them, his belief being that a good neighbor feels responsible for the welfare of those around it. At Kingston, Ontario, in August, 1938, he declared that the United States would not "stand idly by" if Canada were threatened with invasion. It was impossible for the President to attend the Pan-American Conference at Lima, Peru, in 1936 (see Chapter 13). He sent Secretary Cordell Hull to represent him and the United States at Lima. Secretary Hull told the delegates there that the Americas wished to maintain good relations with the rest of the world but that they wished also to preserve their own way of life. He emphasized the right of small nations to remain independent and to keep their liberty. The Conference, through its delegates, adopted resolutions stating that the Americas would stand together against aggression —and German aggression was in the minds of those who voted.

President Roosevelt sent Under-Secretary of State Sumner Welles to represent him and the United States at Panama, in 1939. The Declaration of Panama, passed by the delegates in attendance, was another warning by North and South America of their intention to protect themselves. It established a 300-mile safety belt around the hemisphere within which war activities were banned. Though the warring countries would

A happy family group. President and Mrs. Roosevelt with their numerous grandchildren.

not recognize the safety belt, yet the Americas held to their declaration that ships of Germany and Italy should not come within the belt.

Foreign affairs changed and defense increased. "Peace through preparedness" was the motto of the President and his chief advisers. Under the President's leadership there was planned a large army and navy, with many more airplanes and pilots. Congress passed huge appropriations of money to pay for them.

And yet, in spite of these warlike preparations, the President continued his efforts for a world in which peace would prevail and differences should not be settled by force. He made clear that the United States would take part in creating such a world, and he used the power of his office as well as his personal talents toward this end.

In the uneasy world of June 1939, the rulers of Great Britain, King George VI and Queen Elizabeth, came to the United States to pay a visit. They had been invited by President and Mrs. Roosevelt, who met them at the Pennsylvania station in Washington and greeted them as cordially as the Roosevelts welcomed all guests. In the ride up Pennsylvania Avenue to the White House, the King rode with the President, while Queen Elizabeth followed in a second car with Mrs. Roosevelt. The procession, honoring the King and Queen, gave a hint of the increasing military strength of the United States. There were grim armed tanks and troops of cavalry. Soldiers, sailors, and marines lined the streets of the route in a solid wall. Airplanes—the powerful new "flying fortresses" as well as smaller pursuit planes—flew overhead with a mighty roar. The President, as Commander-in-Chief of the armed forces, was proud to have a visiting ruler see the might of this country.

One morning during their visit the President personally took the King and the Queen on a sightseeing tour of Washington. He showed them the sights familiar to every visitor—the Lincoln Memorial, Mt. Vernon, Arlington, and other places—but probably few other people have had the President of the United States as a guide to Washington.

After entertaining the visitors formally in Washington at the White House, the President and Mrs. Roosevelt next entertained them informally at Hyde Park over the week-end. On Sunday morning, with the President and Mrs. Roosevelt, King George and Queen Elizabeth attended service at tiny, old St. James Episcopal Church, where the Roosevelts had worshiped for years and where the President was senior warden. After church there was a typical Roosevelt picnic luncheon outdoors on the slope of Dutchess Hill in front of the President's new cottage. The King ate "hot dogs" and asked for more; he went swimming with the President in his private pool; and in the afternoon the President himself drove the King and the Queen around the estate to show them his forestry plantings and his other farm crops. The Queen charmed everyone. The President said, when the rulers left on Sunday night, "Well, there go two nice young people."

The King and Queen were safely back in England when the world storm broke. At 2:50 A.M. on September 1st 1939 the telephone by the President's bedside at the White House rang. He knew the call was of immense importance, or he would not have been awakened at that hour. The voice at the other end of the wire came across the Atlantic Ocean.

"Mr. President, the Germans are bombing the cities of Poland," said William C. Bullitt, American Ambassador to France. He was speaking from Paris. "Anthony Biddle (American Minister to Poland) has just called me."

"May God help us all," answered the President solemnly. Bombs meant death and war, as he knew only too well.

At once he began telephoning his Cabinet members who were in Washington and other advisers to meet to discuss the world disaster. The group must decide what additional measures the United States could take to stay out of the conflict. By breakfast time the President had made a plea to the countries involved—Germany, Poland, Britain, France and Italy—that they refrain from bombing unfortified cities and noncombatants (the people who were not fighting). Each country promptly replied that it would obey this request provided the others did; nevertheless, the bombing continued.

That day the President pledged to the people of the United States that he would do all in his power to keep this nation out of war and at peace. He said he hoped and believed it could be done.

On Sunday, September 3rd, Germany, Great Britain, and France were at war; and World War II had started.

The last week in September 1939, the President addressed Congress. He was grave, none of his usual jollity in evidence. He requested the repeal of the embargo preventing the shipment of United States arms to countries at war. It was evident now, he told Congress, that the embargo was hurting Great Britain and France by withholding needed help from them while it helped Germany. During his speech, the diplomatic representatives of Germany and Italy were absent from the gallery of the House of Representatives.

In early June France surrendered to Germany and the world situation became even more acute.

Also in June President Roosevelt did an unusual thing. He needed Secretaries of the Navy and of War. In times of war the defense of the country depends upon these two officials; he wished, therefore, to select men who were especially fitted for the jobs. He saw two such men in the Republican party. They were Frank Knox and Henry L. Stimson. He asked Mr. Knox to become Secretary of the Navy and Mr. Stimson to become Secretary of War, and he sent their names to Congress for approval. There was some argument in Congress over whether a Democratic President should choose Republicans for his Cabinet, but Congress approved the nominations and the new Secretaries took over their important jobs.

As the dictator nations became more powerful and subdued more free peoples, the world situation increased in gravity. It became evident that more soldiers were needed than the small regular army which the United States had always maintained. In August 1940, the President asked Congress for authority to mobilize, or call out, the National Guard for one year as a step in the defense of this country. After debate in Congress, this was passed.

But the National Guard, with the regular army of peace times, was not large enough to defend the United States if the necessity arose. A vastly larger regular army was needed. The United States had not wanted to become a military nation nor did it favor drafting men in times of peace to serve in the Army. Yet, because of the threatened danger abroad, it appeared necessary to draft men so that all young men should share equally in the sacrifice entailed in defending America. The draft was also protection against war. Trained soldiers are more able defenders than untrained ones, and warlike nations respect a country that is prepared to protect its rights.

In September 1940 Congress passed the Selective Service Training Act known as the Draft Bill. By it, 16,500,000 men, aged 21 to 36, became liable for compulsory military service for one year. It was the first peacetime draft in American history and it became a law when it was signed by the President on September 15th. Standing directly behind him when he signed was a small group most directly concerned with the defense program. The group included Secretary Stimson, members of the House and Senate Committees on Military Affairs, and General George C. Marshall, Chief of Staff of the Army. Immediately after signing the bill the President issued a proclamation, in addition to a statement explaining how the 16,500,000 men should be handled.

"America stands at the cross-roads of its destiny," he said in his proclamation. "Time and distances are shortened. A few weeks have seen great nations fall. We can not remain indifferent to the philosophy of force now rampant in the world. The terrible fate of nations whose weakness invited attack is known to us all.

"We must and will marshal our great potential strength to fend off war from our shores. We must and will prevent our land from becoming a victim of aggression . . .

"After thoughtful deliberation, and as the first step, our young men will come from the factories and the fields, the cities and the towns, to enroll their names on registration day.

"On that eventful day my generation will salute their generation. May we all renew within our hearts that conception of liberty and that way of life which we have inherited; may we strengthen our resolve to hold high the torch of freedom in this darkening world so that our children and their children may not be robbed of their rightful inheritance."

On October 16th the men were registered at their local voting precincts. Each one filled out a blank giving his name, age, occupation, and address. On October 29th the draft began and the first number called was 158. Soon men began to report at the camps and forts that sprang up like cities all over the country.

Besides the men drafted, there had to be guns, planes, and ships—all the machines of war—in vast quantities. There had to be enough of them produced for our own use and also enough to help Great Britain. The appropriations ran into billions of dollars. Never before had the United States planned so great a program for the making of war. The war industries employed many workers, thus reducing the number of unemployed. This realized a hope of the President for a job for every person, but he had certainly not desired it to come through the horrors of war.

CHAPTER FIFTEEN

ELECTION AND THIRD INAUGURATION

In the midst of preparation for protection in a world of war came the presidential election year of 1940. The Democratic and the Republican parties began to talk of candidates and again, as in 1916, a European war loomed as a campaign issue. National politics were further tangled by the fact that President Roosevelt would not state whether he would run for a third term. He declared that "he had no wish to be a candidate again," but he refused to say whether he would serve, if elected. He kept his plans to himself. He declined to start presidential politics going at full blast inside the Democratic party when he was making supreme efforts to achieve a united country. He was, he said, President of the United States and he was sticking close to the affairs of the nation, as his position required. A "Draft Roosevelt" movement was begun that spread all over the country.

He would not go to the National Democratic Convention held at Chicago in mid-July. However, he was chosen on the first ballot. Henry A. Wallace, Secretary of Agriculture, was nominated for the Vice-Presidency with him.

In his radio speech of acceptance of the nomination, President Roosevelt said it had been his intention to

**The President often drove his own car at Hyde Park. With him is
Prime Minister McKenzie King of Canada.**

retire at the end of his second term. But the world
conflict had made it unwise to issue a public statement
as to his intentions beforehand lest he injure the influence of the United States in its efforts to prevent the
spread of war. He said further, "Lying awake, as I
have on many nights, I have asked myself whether I
have the right, as Commander-in-Chief of the Army
and Navy, to call on men and women to serve their
country or to train themselves to serve and, at the same
time, decline to serve my country in my own personal
capacity if I am called upon to do so by the people
of the country . . . In the face of any danger that
confronts our times, no individual retains, or can hope

to retain, the right of personal choice which free men enjoy in times of peace." Only the people can draft a President, he continued. "If such a draft should be made upon me, I say, in all simplicity, I will, with God's help, continue to serve with the best of my ability and the fullness of my strength."

The Republicans had already nominated Wendell L. Willkie as their candidate for the Presidency, and he and Franklin Roosevelt were pitted against each other.

Controversy raged over the third-term issue. No law forbade an American President to serve more than two terms, but on the other hand no President had ever done it. Therefore, through the years, tradition had been built up against a President's running for a third term. The country took sides and argued violently. There were people who argued that the United States would surely go to pieces if the third-term tradition were broken. Others maintained that the United States would be much more likely to go to pieces if a new and untried President guided foreign affairs in the world crisis. The latter side felt that precedents were being broken all over the world. Why not break an old and useless tradition by keeping Franklin Roosevelt as President, provided he would accept? His wisdom and experience, gained through eight years, were needed. Hadn't he broken precedents all his life? An old saying, "it is bad luck to swap horses in mid-stream," was quoted by those people who wanted the President to be elected.

"I am an old campaigner and I love a good fight!"

President Roosevelt declared in a campaign address he made at Philadelphia after his nomination. His conduct both before and during the campaign showed that he was indeed a veteran campaigner and a most successful one. People who were opposed to him for the third term declared that his ability to get votes was due to the vast government spending under the New Deal. It had made him immensely popular with the needy people who were helped by the New Deal, his opponents asserted.

However, Franklin Roosevelt was a successful vote-getter long before there was a New Deal. An unknown youngster, he had been elected to the senate of New York State by his personal popularity, his earnestness, his ability and his total disregard of political bosses. When he had run for the Vice-Presidency on the national ticket with James M. Cox, he attracted crowds wherever he spoke even though he did not win. Again, in 1924, his popularity was shown during the turbulent Democratic Convention that met in New York City; angry delegates, supporters of Al Smith and of William G. McAdoo, forgot their wrath and went wild with delight every time Franklin Roosevelt, on crutches, appeared on the platform. Moreover, he had been elected a Democratic Governor of New York State in a year when a Republican, Herbert Hoover, won the Presidency. All of this showed that he had usually been able to convince the people of his fitness for public office without the New Deal. So, in 1940, Franklin Roosevelt fought his usual good fight, through speeches in person and on the radio. As usual, when

President Roosevelt, his wife and mother driving to vote at Hyde Park.

others around him grew weary, he seemed to take on new life and vigor.

When election day rolled around, Mr. Roosevelt went, as was his habit, to Hyde Park to vote and to await the results. With his wife and mother, he rode into the village of Hyde Park on November 5th to cast his ballot. Many old friends greeted him as he entered the Town Hall, where the voting took place. His number in the election book was 611.

"Your name?" asked the young married woman who was chairman of the election board. She was required to ask this routine question in the discharge of her duty.

"Franklin D. Roosevelt," he answered as if he had been any unknown citizen. He cast his vote very quickly while photographers made pictures of him before, while, and after he voted.

He then returned to his mother's home, Hyde Park House, to keep up with the election returns coming in from all over the United States. He soon found that he had been elected by a big electoral vote.

Just before midnight, long lines of lights bobbed like huge candles along the avenue leading from the highway to Hyde Park House. These were lines of people carrying flares and moving in a torchlight procession. It had been a custom for years to celebrate Democratic victories by organizing a parade to Hyde Park House and this year the local people had an especial reason to be proud; Franklin Roosevelt had broken an American tradition and was the first President to be elected for a third time. Friends and neighbors had only waited until the returns made them sure of his election before setting out to congratulate Mr. Roosevelt.

As he had done twice before, the President stood on the front porch to welcome the crowd. He leaned on the arm of his third son, Franklin, Jr., and beamed at the crowd before him. The town band stopped playing. He began to speak.

"We are facing difficult days in this country," he told the throng, "but I think you will find me in the future the same Franklin Roosevelt you have always known."

On January 20th, 1941, Franklin Delano Roosevelt

became President for a third term, the first American to be so honored. He was within ten days of being 59 years of age.

The long day of ceremonies began with religious worship, as had each of Mr. Roosevelt's former inaugurations. A brief service, lasting about fifteen minutes, was held at 10:30 in the morning at historic St. John's Church, known as the Church of the Presidents. There was no sermon.

As he drove down Pennsylvania Avenue in an open car on his way to the Capitol and the inauguration, he was in high spirits. He chatted with Speaker Rayburn of the House of Representatives, who sat beside him, and he waved his high silk hat to the thousands of people who jammed the sidewalks along the way. The eyes of those thousands were fastened on him as if he alone knew whether peace or war lay ahead.

Arriving at the Capitol, Henry A. Wallace was sworn in as Vice-President. The Constitutional oath was then given the President by Chief Justice Hughes. The President took it with his hand on the same family Bible which he had used in both former inaugurations. One hundred thousand people crowded in the vast open space before the platform and shivered in the clear, bitter air while they listened to the President's address. In spite of the intense cold, the President spoke bareheaded and he spoke as seriously as if he were preaching a sermon.

His speech was broadcast throughout the world. In it he considered the condition, the strength and the future of free democracies in the threatened world.

He compared the trials before this country to those
endured by the American people in the days of Washington and Lincoln. He urged the unity of American
citizens before the common foe. He called the country
to the defense of democracy. He said, in part:

"In the face of great perils never before encountered,
our strong purpose is to protect and to perpetuate the
integrity of democracy.

"For this we muster the spirit of America, and the
faith of America."

He ended:

"We do not retreat. We are not content to stand
still. As Americans, we go forward, in the service of
our country, by the will of God."

His speech brought to mind President Woodrow
Wilson's first inaugural address in which he eloquently
declared: "This is not a day of triumph: it is a day
of dedication." The two prayers in the inauguration
ceremonies, an invocation and a benediction, were for
peace. People listened hopefully but fearfully lest the
peace of the United States soon be shattered.

After the inauguration President Roosevelt em-
braced John Nance Garner, his former Vice-President.
The President, who had once called Mr. Garner "Old
Man Commonsense," wished him Godspeed on his
journey back home to Texas.

Mrs. Roosevelt rode back to the White House beside
the President. Sixteen Roosevelts of four generations
had sat on the rostrum and watched the President take
the oath of office. His 86-year-old mother had patted

him on the back as she passed him on her way back to her car.

President and Mrs. Roosevelt entertained 1,000 guests for luncheon immediately after the inauguration. The President then reviewed the parade. It featured the preparedness program of the United States and showed the new military power that this country was getting ready to use in defense of democracies, if necessary. In former parades at inaugurations, there had been the bright colors of dress uniforms, many floats, drum majors and "majorettes," and silk-hatted men marching from the states. This year the frills and furbelows were gone, as well as the color. Drab, warlike khaki and sober Navy blue were the colors, worn by soldiers, sailors and marines. Young men from West Point and Annapolis marched. Tanks rolled by. Monster planes, 200 of them, roared and zoomed overhead. Soldiers wore steel helmets for field service and marched with fixed bayonets.

Crowds estimated at 500,000 persons were on the streets to see the parade. The crowds were serious, as if they felt the solemnity of the occasion and what such a military parade meant in changing the American way of life. Only 48 hours before the inauguration, Hitler and Mussolini had met to plan new moves— Hitler to outline greater conquests and Mussolini to demand more help. The military parade also reminded the crowd that 1,000,000 men had been called to service and that enormous sums of money were being spent for defense.

After the parade was over, 2,500 guests were invited to tea at the White House. A family dinner of 40 guests closed the day for the President and Mrs. Roosevelt. Mrs. Roosevelt was beginning her ninth year in the White House and it was a strenuous day for her in planning food for a total of 3,500 people besides her own family. Like the President, she enjoyed guests, even in such large numbers.

FRIENDSHIPS AND DAILY LIFE

There are always burdens to the office of the Presidency, even when the President was a gay, cheerful person like Franklin Roosevelt. Some Presidents have been broken by the strain. Franklin Roosevelt bore the burdens wonderfully. The later coming of war, first to Europe, and on December 7th, 1941 to the United States, increased them considerably and gave Mr. Roosevelt longer working hours than any other President of recent times ever had.

Unless he had been awakened earlier by some emergency, President Roosevelt's day usually began around 8:30 each morning. He breakfasted in bed on scrambled eggs, bacon, toast and milk and quickly scanned several newspapers before his secretaries appeared with the list of people he must see as well as the most important mail. He was wheeled to the Executive Offices around 10:30. First, he attacked the huge pile of mail and documents piled on his desk. He read very rapidly, almost a page at a glance, except military and State papers which he read slowly and carefully. From the time he arrived until late afternoon he had a steady stream of callers. Most of them came to discuss war matters. Interviews with Mr. Roosevelt were for fifteen minutes, but he was so interested in each subject presented to him that he was quite likely to ask many questions and keep his caller longer than the scheduled time. Thus, his secretaries had a hard time adhering to the day's schedule.

In order to lose no time, lunch was served at his desk. Visitors often lunched with him and talked while they ate. He did not leave his office until around 5:30 in the afternoon, or even as late as six. He used to take time to swim in the White House pool before dinner but after war started he seldom did, owing to the pressure of heavy work; and if he did swim, he took business callers along to continue important conversations; so he did not relax after all.

After dinner he went to his study on the second floor of the White House and worked over papers he must sign until around midnight. During the night the phone by his bed might ring, bringing important news about the war situation. Except for occasional cruises at sea, week-ends at Hyde Park were his only rest, though, since his mother's death in September 1941, he had not gone there so often; however, there he could catch up on sleep, enjoy sitting on the front porch like any other individual, drive his own car around the countryside, and relax. What citizen would like to exchange working hours with an American President, and particularly a war President?

A man who carries the burdens of the Presidency needs a trusted friend. He needs a friend on whom he can depend for candid advice as well as a friend who thinks as he does. Such a devoted friend was Louis Howe. His death left a gap in Mr. Roosevelt's life that was hard to fill. Gradually Mr. Roosevelt came to depend more and more on Harry Hopkins. Mr. Roosevelt and Mr. Hopkins had been friends for years and years. Mr. Hopkins was a social worker by profession. While Mr. Roosevelt was Governor of New York State, he knew young Mr. Hopkins, who held executive offices in social work. When Mr. Roosevelt became President, one of his early acts was to choose Harry Hopkins to head the new Federal Emergency Relief Administration, known by its initials as the F.E.R.A. Mr. Hopkins believed passionately that help was needed by people who were out of work because there were not enough jobs to go around and so he did his best as head of the F.E.R.A. He and the President saw eye to eye in this need of jobs, and that deepened their friendship.

Later Harry Hopkins was appointed Secretary of Commerce and thus became a member of the Cabinet.

In May 1940, the President sent for Mr. Hopkins to spend a week-end at the White House and he remained there. The President would not let him leave. In August 1940, Mr. Hopkins resigned as Secretary of Commerce on account of ill health, but he still made his home at the White House, even after he later married again. When he resigned, the President wrote him:

"Dear Harry: You may resign the office—only the office—and nothing else. Our friendship will and must go on as always."

Because he was not well, Mr. Hopkins had to rest a great deal. But he was "on call" whenever the President wanted him, day or night, so that he was always

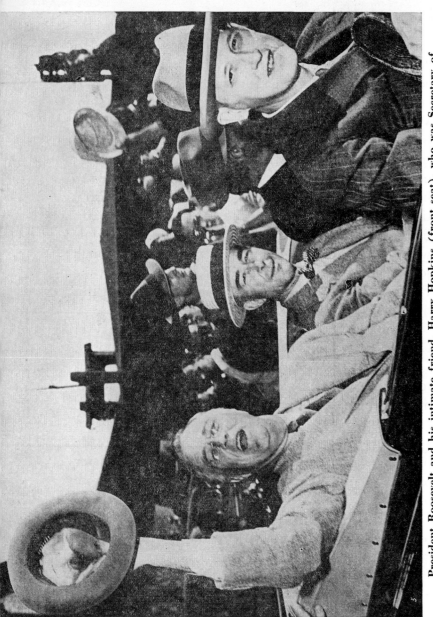

President Roosevelt and his intimate friend, Harry Hopkins (front seat), who was Secretary of Commerce and "on call" whenever the President wanted him, day or night.

near. He went on trips with the President: cruises along the Potomac, week-end trips to Hyde Park, trips across the Atlantic on confidential missions after war came. "Send for Harry" was the President's command to his secretaries when he wanted something important done. And Harry Hopkins generally got it done. He was a doer as well as a crusader.

A President needs diversion as well as friends to help him take his mind off his problems. Fala, a Scottish terrier known as a Scotty, became Mr. Roosevelt's pet dog in November 1940. While Mr. Roosevelt played with Fala, he forgot for a moment the burdens of his high office.

Fala slept in Mr. Roosevelt's bedroom at night. He met distinguished visitors who called at the White House. He went everywhere with the President. He traveled back and forth to Hyde Park; he sat on the seat beside his master when Mr. Roosevelt drove his own small car at Hyde Park. He even went to sea with the President.

Mr. Roosevelt had a wide circle of unseen friends to whom he talked by radio. They were the people of this nation. "Fireside chats" Mr. Roosevelt called them because he liked to think of the citizens of the United States as sitting comfortably by their firesides listening while he talked to them about the state of the nation. He was the first leader in public life to realize the value of the radio. On Sunday evening, December 29th, 1940, Mr. Roosevelt made one of his "fireside chats," and this particular one was about the dangers of war coming close to the United States. He

While Mr. Roosevelt played with Fala, his pet dog, he forgot for a
moment the burdens of his high office.

said, among other things, "Never before since James-
town and Plymouth Rock has our American civilization been in such danger as now. . . . We have no
excuse for defeatism. We have every good reason for
hope—hope for peace, yes, and hope for the defense
of our civilization and for the building of a better civilization for the future.

". . . I have the profound conviction that the American people are determined to put forth a mightier
effort than they have ever yet made to increase our
production of all the implements of defense to meet
the threat to our democratic faith. As President of the
United States, I call for that national effort. I call for
it in the name of this nation which we love and honor
and are privileged and proud to serve. I call on our
people with absolute confidence that our common
sense will succeed."

More than 100 years before, President Monroe had
formulated our foreign policy, now known as the Monroe Doctrine. He said the United States would regard
it as an unfriendly act for any foreign power to secure
and hold territory in this hemisphere. President Roosevelt reaffirmed this policy, saying we were determined
that the oceans adjoining our coasts should not be
controlled by any foreign power which opposes with
violence our way of life and will destroy it.

President Roosevelt's speech, which the *New York
Times* called "one of the historic landmarks of American history," had another happy personal effect, for
it and the threat of war brought Al Smith and the
President together in friendship again. Al Smith, who

had opposed Mr. Roosevelt's third term, said on his sixty-seventh birthday, December 30th, 1940, that he thought the President's speech was "a very courageous, hard-hitting speech" and that he was in hearty accord with it.

But in spite of Mr. Roosevelt's hopes, and the hopes of all Americans, war hovered very near the shores of this continent.

CHAPTER SEVENTEEN

THE FOUR FREEDOMS

During his long term of office, President Roosevelt made many important speeches. Perhaps none of them is better remembered and more widely quoted than a message to Congress, which he delivered in person in January 1941. In the latter part of the speech, he stated that the future security of the world should be founded on four human freedoms—freedom of speech, freedom of worship, freedom from want, freedom from fear. Although the United States was not yet involved in the European war, and did not enter it until the following December, Mr. Roosevelt saw that this country would inevitably be drawn into it. He therefore thought it essential to state what should result from a global war. TIME MAGAZINE, in reporting the speech, said: "Mr. Roosevelt spoke as clearly as ever, but there was no lightness in his voice, no touch of humor. As he went on, his big head thrown back, his voice gained depth and strength and emotion."

Here is the speech:

> "At no previous time has American security been as seriously threatened from without as it is today. . . . . Today, thank God, 130,000,000 Americans, in 48 states, have forgotten points of the compass in national unity. . . .
>
> "We need not overemphasize imperfections in the

peace of Versailles. We need not harp on failure of the democracies to deal with problems of world reconstruction. We should remember that the peace of 1919 was far less unjust than the kind of 'pacification' which began even before Munich, and which is being carried on under the new order of tyranny which seeks to spread over every continent today. . . .

"As your President, . . . I find it necessary to report that the future and the safety of our country and our democracy are overwhelmingly involved in events far beyond our borders.

"Armed defense of democratic existence is now being gallantly waged in four continents. If that defense fails, all the population and all the resources of Europe, Asia, Africa and Australia will be dominated by the conquerors. . . .

"In times like these it is immature—and incidentally untrue—for anybody to brag that an unprepared America, singlehanded and with one hand tied behind its back, can hold off the entire world.

"No realistic American can expect from a dictator's peace international generosity, or return of true independence, or world disarmament, or freedom of expression, or freedom of religion—or even good business.

"Such a peace would bring no security for us or our neighbors. 'Those who would give up essential liberty to purchase little temporary safety deserve neither liberty nor safety.' . . .

"We must especially beware of that small group of selfish men who would clip the wings of the American eagle in order to feather their own nests. . . .

"We must learn from the lessons of the past years in Europe—particularly the lesson of Norway. . . . The first phase of the invasion of this hemisphere would not be the landing of regular troops. The necessary strategic points would be occupied by secret agents and their dupes—and great numbers of them are already here and in Latin America. . . .

"Our national policy is this: First, by an impressive expression of the public will and without regard to partisanship, we are committed to an all-inclusive national defense.

"Second, by an impressive expression of the public will and without regard to partisanship, we are committed to full support of all those resolute peoples, everywhere, who are resisting aggression and are thereby keeping war away from our hemisphere. . . .

"Third, by an impressive expression of the public will and without regard to partisanship, we are committed to the proposition that principles of morality and considerations for our own security will never permit us to acquiesce in a peace dictated by aggressors and sponsored by appeasers. . . .

"Therefore, the immediate need is a swift and driving increase in our armament production. . . . I am not satisfied with the progress thus far made. . . . None of us will be satisfied until the job is done.

"I shall ask this Congress for greatly increased new appropriations and authorizations to carry on what we have begun. I also ask this Congress for authority and for funds sufficient to manufacture additional munitions and war supplies of many kinds, to be turned over to those nations which are now in actual war with aggressor nations.

"Let us say to the democracies: 'We Americans are vitally concerned in your defense of freedom. We are putting forth our energies, our resources and our organized powers to give you the strength to regain and maintain a free world. We shall send you, in ever-increasing numbers, ships, planes, tanks, guns. This is our purpose and our pledge.'

"In fulfillment of this purpose, we will not be intimidated by the threats of dictators that they will regard as a breach of international law and as an act of war our aid to the democracies which dare to resist their aggression. Such aid is not an act of war, even if a dictator should unilaterally program it so to be.

"When the dictators are ready to make war upon us, they will not wait for an act of war on our part. . . .

"Their only interest is in a new one-way international law. . . .

"We must all prepare to make the sacrifices that the emergency—as serious as war itself—demands. . . .

"As men do not live by bread alone, they do not fight by armaments alone. Those who man our defenses and those behind them who build our defenses must have the stamina and courage which come from an unshakable belief in the manner of life they are defending. The mighty action which we are calling for can not be based on a disregard of all things worth fighting for. . . .

"The basic things expected by our people of their political and economic systems are simple. They are:

"Equality of opportunity for youth and for others.

"Jobs for those who can work.

"Security for those who need it.

"The ending of special privilege for the few.

"The preservation of civil liberties for all.

"The enjoyment of the fruits of scientific progress in a wider and constantly rising standard of living. . . .

"I have called for personal sacrifices. I am assured of the willingness of almost all Americans to respond to that call.

"In the future days, which we seek to make secure, we look forward to a world founded on four essential human freedoms.

"The first is freedom of speech and expression—everywhere in the world.

"The second is freedom of every person to worship God in his own way—everywhere in the world.

"The third is freedom from want—which, translated into world terms, means economic understandings which will secure to every nation a healthy peacetime life for its inhabitants—everywhere in the world.

"The fourth is freedom from fear—which, translated into world terms, means a worldwide reduction of armaments to such a point and in such a thorough fashion that no nation will be in a position to commit an act of physical aggression against any neighbor —anywhere in the world. . . .

"Freedom means the supremacy of human rights everywhere. Our support goes to those who struggle to gain those rights or keep them. Our strength is in our unity of purpose.

"To that high concept there can be no end save victory."

CHAPTER EIGHTEEN

A WAR PRESIDENT

President Roosevelt loved to do unexpected and surprising things. He loved to astonish people. He had done one totally unexpected and surprising thing when, in the summer of 1932, he flew to Chicago to accept the Democratic nomination for the Presidency. During the summer following his third inauguration he did another equally surprising thing. In August 1941, he slipped away from Washington very quietly without the public's knowledge of his absence.

War clouds were then rolling closer and closer to the peace-loving United States. If war came to America President Roosevelt felt that the United States and Great Britain should formulate and state publicly the war aims of these two countries. He felt that this could be done better if Winston Churchill, Prime Minister of Great Britain, and he talked matters over face to face. So he left to meet Prime Minister Churchill for a conference.

He did not even let the high-ranking officers of his staff who went with him know where they were going. General George Marshall, Chief of Staff of the Army, had planned to give a small dinner party on an August night at his home at nearby Fort Myers. The very afternoon of the dinner General Marshall telephoned

his wife that he had received sudden orders to leave
town with his destination unknown; Mrs. Marshall did
not know of his whereabouts until much later when
she read about the meeting in the papers. President
Roosevelt's son Elliott was another surprised person.
Then a captain in the Army Air Forces and on duty
in Newfoundland, Elliott thought he was in disgrace
when he was ordered not to leave his station; he did
not know any better until he was told to fly out over
the water and he saw his father and all the important
people who had come with the President.

Fala, the black Scotty, went along, too, as well as the
important people. Fala was a good sailor. He did not
mind when the sea became very rough, and he had to
be kept on a leash for fear he would fall overboard. His
master, the President, was far too busy to pay him much
attention, but other people looked after the friendly
little dog. And some way or other Fala managed to be
included in the photograph of the leaders made just
before the meeting ended; he looked like a ragged
black mop lying at the feet of President Roosevelt.

The meeting took place at sea somewhere off the
coast of Newfoundland. President Roosevelt was on
the U. S. cruiser *Augusta.* Prime Minister Churchill
and his party were on the much larger British ship of
35,000 tons, the *Prince of Wales,* on which they had
crossed the Atlantic Ocean. An escort of cruisers and
destroyers formed a fleet large enough to fight a sea
battle, if one became necessary. Patrol planes on guard
flew overhead constantly.

Day after day, with gray fog around them most of

The Atlantic Charter was formulated during a meeting at sea, August 1941, between President Roosevelt, left, and Prime Minister Winston Churchill, right, front row. Behind them stand, left to right, Admiral King, General Marshall, and Field Marshall Dill.

the time, President Roosevelt, Prime Minister Churchill, and their staffs talked and planned together. It was the first time that a President of the United States and a Prime Minister of Great Britain had met at sea to talk over matters of importance. And there was a great deal to talk about. The United States did not want to be drawn into war. It wanted nothing except the right to live peacefully with the rest of the world. Germany was already at war with England. England was our mother country; we spoke the same language; we had the same ideals. We wished to tell the world how we felt jointly. President Roosevelt and his advisers, and Prime Minister Churchill and his advisers, went over the world situation. They considered with care what had better be said.

All meetings were held on the *Augusta* except Sunday church service. On Sunday morning the *Augusta* pulled alongside the mighty *Prince of Wales*. President Roosevelt crossed over to attend divine services held on the *Wales'* deck. Together with guests, officers and crews of both vessels, President Roosevelt and Prime Minister Churchill sang the hymns lustily and listened to the chaplain preach.

At the end of the conference, a statement known as the Atlantic Charter was issued. Signed by both President Roosevelt and Prime Minister Churchill, the Atlantic Charter contained eight points. The first point said, in plain, unmistakable language, that the United States and Great Britain "sought no aggrandisement, territorial or otherwise;" and the third point stated that both countries, the United States and Great

Britain, "respect the rights of all people to choose the form of government under which they will live." That last statement seemed almost unnecessary to citizens of the United States who have always had that right. However, it heartened the people of Europe, particularly the people of the small countries that were being drawn into the war against their will.

After his return to England, Mr. Churchill said publicly that the purpose of the Atlantic Charter and its eight points was "To give hope and the assurance of final victory to those many scores of men and women who are battling for life and freedom or who are already bent down under the Nazi yoke."

Because it has become one of the great documents in the development of the world, it is given here as President Roosevelt included it in a message to Congress:

> "The President and the Prime Minister have had several conferences. They have considered the dangers to world civilization arising from the policies of military domination by conquest upon which the Hitlerite government of Germany and other governments associated therewith have embarked, and have made clear the steps which their countries are respectively taking for their safety in the face of these dangers.
>
> "They have agreed on the following joint declaration:
>
> "Joint declaration of the President of the United States and Prime Minister Churchill, Mr. Churchill representing His Majesty's government in the United Kingdom, being met together, deem it right to make known certain common principles in the national policies of their respective countries on which they

base their hopes for a better future for the world:

THE ATLANTIC CHARTER

"1. Their countries seek no aggrandisement, territorial or otherwise;

"2. They desire to see no territorial changes that do not accord with the freely expressed wishes of the peoples concerned;

"3. They respect the right of all people to choose the form of government under which they will live; and they wish to see sovereign rights and self-government restored to those who have been forcibly deprived of them;

"4. They will endeavor, with due respect for their existing obligations, to further the enjoyment of all states, great and small, victor and vanquished, of access, on equal terms, to the trade and to the raw materials of the world which are needed for their economic security;

"5. They desire to bring about the fullest collaboration between all nations in the economic field with the object of securing, for all, improved labor standards, economic advancement, and social security;

"6. After the final destruction of the Nazi tyranny, they hope to see established a peace which will afford to all nations the means of dwelling in safety within their own boundaries, and which will afford assurance that all the men in all the lands may live out their lives in freedom from fear and want;

"7. Such a peace will enable all men to traverse the high seas and oceans without hindrance;

"8. They believe that all nations of the world, for spiritual reasons, must come to the abandonment of the use of force. Since no future peace can be maintained if land, sea, or air armaments continue to be employed by nations which threaten, or may threaten, aggression outside their frontiers, they believe, pending the establishment of a wider and more permanent system of general security, that the disarmament of such nations is essential. They will likewise aid and encourage all other practical measures which will lighten for peace-loving people the crushing burden of armaments.

Signed:
Franklin D. Roosevelt,
Winston Churchill."

An anxious Fall followed. The United States was doing its best to keep out of a shooting war. President Roosevelt, as leader, was using every honorable means to avoid being drawn into it. And then the dreaded blow fell.

"THE JAPS HAVE ATTACKED US AT PEARL HARBOR!"

This alarming news flash came over the radio on the afternoon of December 7th, 1941. People all over this country were relaxing comfortably and listening to the radio after their Sunday dinner. At first they could not believe their ears. It seemed incredible that Japan would dare attack the mighty United States. But it was only too true. As President Roosevelt had predicted in his message to Congress the preceding January, "When the dictators are ready to make war upon us, they will not wait for an act of war on our part." This proved to be correct. Without warning, the Japs had taken the United States by surprise.

"Fight back!" the President ordered the Army and Navy.

He immediately went into action. He called a Cabi-

net meeting for 8:30 that Sunday night. In his study
on the second floor of the White House he talked first
to the members of his Cabinet, then to the Congres-
sional leaders. When he had finished with these two
groups, he went back to work. There were many orders
to be given. His speech for the next day must be prepared. At last toward daylight, he went to bed for a
little sleep. At noon the next day he got in the big
black closed White House car and was driven to the
Capitol. Extra precautions were taken to guard him.
On each running board of his car stood a Secret Service man. On either side of his car were open Secret
Service cars, three men on each running board, four
men inside each car. The men outside held sawed-off
riot guns. Those inside carried .38 calibre service re-
volvers. These men scanned the streets, their keen eyes
alert for any danger that might threaten the President.

The Capitol was equally well guarded. Police, Marines, plain-clothes men were stationed both outside
and inside along the corridors.

The House of Representatives was packed with con-
gressmen and senators, members of the Cabinet and
the Supreme Court. The President stood just below
the Stars and Stripes on the wall. His usual ready smile
was gone. He looked grim. His big shoulders were
square, the lines in his face deeper. Facing the tense
throng, he said:

"Yesterday, December 7th, 1941—a date that will
live in infamy—the United States of America was suddenly and deliberately attacked by naval and air forces
of Japan. The attack yesterday . . . caused severe dam-

age to the American naval and military forces . . . very many American lives have been lost.

"We will gain the inevitable triumph—so help us God. I ask that the Congress declare a . . . state of war."

Both House and Senate passed the bill declaring war against Japan. At 4:10 that afternoon the President signed it in his office.

Congress followed this action the next day by declaring war against Germany and Italy. Ahead lay war: its sacrifices, disasters, sorrows, heavy taxes to meet the financial cost, its grinding work for every person. The American people, disliking war, yet girded themselves for the grim job.

Heavy responsibilties devolved upon the President. He felt them keenly. It was his duty to get the United States ready to fight this war and to win it. He realized that the future security of the United States lay in victory over these countries and their doctrines. As Commander in Chief, he organized the United States to produce tanks and guns, planes and ships—the necessities of war—in vast quantities as well as to create a vast armed force. All Americans of all political parties had not agreed with Mr. Roosevelt on domestic matters. However, as war leader, he immediately received the unified support of all parties in his war policy.

In order to keep in touch with the progress of the war, at his request, the President was constantly visited by General Marshall, Chief of Staff of the Army; by Admiral Ernest J. King, Commander in Chief of the Fleet and Chief of Naval Operations; by General H. H. ("Hap") Arnold, head of the Army Air Forces; and by other prominent military and naval leaders. Admiral Leahy, retired, became Mr. Roosevelt's aide, or liaison officer, who kept him advised of every happening. New developments were reported to him at once. People who talked to the President were astonished at his official knowledge of war, as if waging it had been his lifelong profession. Because he had been Assistant-Secretary of the Navy during World War I, it had been said that he loved the Navy best on account of his familiarity with it. Yet he soon developed an equally keen interest and knowledge of the methods of ground and air war and became amazingly familiar with all the technical sides of warfare. He completely rejected a defensive policy. He was against keeping our Navy in home waters and our Army in trenches along our coasts, in order to defend America if it were attacked. He said, after Pearl Harbor, "We must go out there, where our enemies are, and fight them on their own home grounds. We must go out and find them and hit them—and hit them again."

President Roosevelt began to have many important visitors from foreign countries as well as our own. Prime Minister Churchill had already paid one visit immediately after Pearl Harbor; he came again and again, crossing the Atlantic almost as easily and as often as if it were a mere river instead of a wide ocean, so that he became a frequent White House guest.

Not only was President Roosevelt the leader of the United States; he was a world leader as well, one of the "big three"—Prime Minister Churchill, Marshal Stalin and himself—on whom the future of the world depended. He insisted on being his own spokesman and, to a great extent, he managed all dealings with foreign nations.

Because he had so many responsibilities, he needed to throw them off sometimes. Playing with Fala was not enough diversion. His only daughter, Anna, Mrs. John Boettiger, saw this need of her father as the war progressed and his burdens increased. Mrs. Boettiger was the "blue-eyed baby," the eldest Roosevelt, who had been born while her father studied law at Columbia University. In December 1943, Mrs. Boettiger came to the White House for a Christmas visit. She had intended to return to Seattle and her job of running a woman's page for a newspaper which her husband had edited before he entered the service. During the Christmas visit she found out two things. One was that her husband would be kept on duty more and more in Washington and she could be with him if she stayed there. She also saw that her father needed her, particularly during her mother's frequent absences. She decided that she and her small son, Johnny—her two older children were away at school—would stay and make their home at the White House.

The special job Mrs. Boettiger took on herself was to try to see that her father did not work so hard nor such long hours. President Roosevelt had always been a terrific worker. The war brought additional burdens and huge problems. So he worked all the harder. All day, every day, he saw one important person after another. He made decisions that affected not only the American people but people all over the world.

After dinner at night he took it easy for a short time, chatting with his family and any guests; then he went to his study on the second floor of the White House and pored over important papers until very late and everyone else was sound asleep.

Mrs. Boettiger did not believe he could maintain this heavy schedule of work without some letup. She began to have lunch with him every day. While he ate, she told him amusing things to make him laugh; she saw to it that he did eat his food, not play with it. She watched over his health. She became an unofficial secretary without salary for her father and did her own typing on a machine in her bedroom. She acted as official hostess when her mother was away. She was a lively, wholesome person, and the President enjoyed her gay companionship.

Mr. Roosevelt's four sons were in service. Though he felt great pride in their records, yet he also carried a personal burden of anxiety concerning them, and thus he knew the anxiety of all parents for their sons who were defending the United States. James, the eldest son, a major and then a lieutenant colonel in the Marines, was decorated repeatedly for bravery, fighting in many Pacific battles. Elliott, the second son, rose to the rank of brigadier general in the Army Air Forces and commanded a reconnaissance unit throughout the fighting in Tunisia, Sicily and Italy. Franklin, Jr., a lieutenant on a destroyer, was decorated for bravery for services in the Mediterranean. John, the youngest, had bad eyesight which disqualified him for combat duty; he served with the Navy supply corps and never ceased trying to get a combat assignment.

Mr. Roosevelt's hair was thinner than when he took office in 1934 and new lines showed in his face. At times he still laughed gaily. He was grim, though, when he talked about what the European nations were suffering and what the United States must do to win the war.

Older and more experienced, he was the same courageous leader who, in March, 1933, told the frightened citizens of the United States that "the only thing we have to fear is fear itself," and the nation forgot its fear in his courage. That was still his belief, that fear was our most deadly enemy.

CHAPTER NINETEEN

A WORLD TRAVELER

President Roosevelt soon began to do an immense amount of world traveling. It was a good thing that he had early formed the habit of constant travel and thus had become accustomed to it. Each summer during his childhood and boyhood he had gone to Europe with his father and mother, traveling over the countries there until he knew some of them almost as well as America. In 1932, during his first campaign for the Presidency, he had traveled across the United States and back again, rolling up a grand total of 17,000 miles. He liked to travel, enjoying every minute of each trip and remaining fresh and enthusiastic when other members of his party were weary. In fact, his friends had declared that travel was a tonic to him; he thrived on it. There had been tremendous improvements in the speed of travel, particularly if a person traveled by air. In a plane, Mr. Roosevelt could eliminate distance almost as swiftly as if he had been whisked around the world by rubbing Aladdin's magic lamp.

It had not been the custom for Presidents of the United States to leave this country while in office lest accident befall them. President Woodrow Wilson changed this custom somewhat when he went to France at the end of World War I. President Wilson's reason for going was in the interest of world peace; hence, the public considered that "peace" was a sufficient cause for his taking the risk involved. However, President Franklin D. Roosevelt did not wait for war to cause him to break this stay-at-home presidential custom. Early in his second term Mr. Roosevelt took time as a "good neighbor" to travel to South America to attend a conference, held at Buenos Aires, of South American countries and the United States. He went there by boat.

Now began his wartime traveling. He traveled far and wide in this country, visiting Army camps. He wanted to see for himself how the millions of young men who had been drafted into the armed forces were being trained at the camps that had sprung up all over the United States.

He also went to foreign lands. It was necessary for the "big three"—himself, Prime Minister Churchill and Marshal Stalin—to talk face to face as to what should be done so that the countries they represented might work and fight together to defeat the enemy. It was also necessary for them and their advisers to map out campaigns and to decide how these three countries could pool their resources.

In January 1943, President Roosevelt started his foreign travel. He again did a totally unexpected thing. No President had ever left this country in war time. No President before him had ever traveled by plane, because of the danger of accident involved. Fear had been left out of Mr. Roosevelt's make-up. He felt it important that he and Prime Minister Churchill should talk over matters again. He did not let the danger involved stop him. Going by way of South America, and using plane, train and auto as his means of travel, he reached Casablanca, on the coast of North Africa. He was about 4,000 miles from Washington. Under tropical palm trees in the grounds of a Casablanca hotel, surrounded by barbed wire and heavy armed guards, President Roosevelt and Prime Minister Churchill conferred for ten days. Each of them occupied a small white villa which was his special headquarters.

Naval and military advisers were with them and met together daily. General Marshall, Admiral King, Harry Hopkins and others accompanied the President. General Eisenhower (General Ike to his soldiers), then commanding the American forces fighting in North Africa, flew to Casablanca at the President's request; General Eisenhower later became Supreme Commander of the Allied Forces in Europe and led them to victory over Germany.

A multitude of problems needed to be discussed at Casablanca. There were military problems, political problems, post-war problems. Here the Sicilian and Italian campaigns were mapped out and the terms of unconditional surrender laid down. The leaders of Russia and China were not present, but Mr. Roosevelt and Mr. Churchill kept in close touch with them.

President Roosevelt visited our troops nearby. About this visit, he told a press conference, "I have seen the bulk of several divisions. I have eaten lunch in the field—and it was a darned good lunch, too."

At the end of the conference an official communiqué was issued. It said, "Complete agreement was reached between the leaders of the two countries and their respective staffs upon war plans and enterprises to be undertaken during 1943 against Germany, Italy and Japan."

After the conference was over, Mr. Roosevelt did not hurry home. He thought it an excellent opportunity to see personally the leaders of other countries. He stopped all along the way; he enjoyed each stop and the new people he met. He paid a visit to Liberia, the only republic in Africa, founded in 1822 as a colony for freed United States slaves. He stopped in Brazil and conferred with its president. The last stop was at Port-au-Spain, the capital of Trinidad. After being away for three weeks, the President's big plane landed at Miami, Florida, on the day after his sixty-first birthday. A special train took him to Washington.

The New York *Times* commented on the trip and his safe return as follows:

"President Roosevelt celebrated his sixty-first birthday . . . at the close of one of the most brilliant episodes of his career; a journey which brought the breath of his democratic enthusiasm into three continents. . . . On a man's birthday we are apt to think of personal things, even when a man is a political figure. Mr. Roosevelt's gaiety and humor, as well as his earnestness, have helped him in his battle. He is a friendly man, at ease equally with a British premier, the President of Brazil, or an American soldier from Kansas or Vermont. He personifies in manner some of democracy's best qualities. The thanks and the prayers of the nation are with him."

President Roosevelt's next trip was just over the line

that bounds the United States on the north. In August, 17th-24th, he met Prime Minister Churchill at Quebec, Canada. Just before the President's train arrived at the siding outside the city where he was to get off, a rainbow shone in the sky after a summer rain. Some of the waiting crowd thought it a sign of good luck. While at Quebec both Mr. Roosevelt and Mr. Churchill lived in The Citadel, a gray fortress on the Plains of Abraham, 300 feet above the St. Lawrence river.

The Quebec conference was mainly a military one. Mr. Roosevelt, Mr. Churchill, and their staffs worked at great pressure. Military events were happening so fast that there were many immediate decisions to be made. Anthony Eden, British Foreign Minister, was there with Mr. Churchill. Present with Mr. Roosevelt were Secretary of State Cordell Hull, Secretary of War Stimson, Secretary of the Navy Knox, and others.

After the Quebec conference ended, Mr. Roosevelt went to Ottawa and spoke to an enormous crowd of Canadians. The speaker's stand on which he stood had been erected on the grounds of the Parliament building. Mr. Roosevelt was deeply impressed by the immense crowd he saw spreading before him and by the enthusiastic welcome it gave him. He said to the crowd, "I shall never forget this day. . . . Sometimes I wish that the great master of intuition, the Nazi leader, could have been present at the Quebec conference. If he and his generals had known our plans, they would have realized that discretion is the better part of valor and that surrender would pay them better now than later." For the benefit of the French-speaking Canadi-

President Roosevelt, center, with Generalissimo and Madam Chiang Kai-shek, at Cairo, Egypt, November, 1943.

ans, he added in French, which he spoke fluently, "Canada is a nation founded on the union of two great races . . . an example everywhere in the world."

Prime Minister Churchill returned to Washington with Mr. Roosevelt for one of the Prime Minister's frequent visits.

In November, 1943, Mr. Roosevelt, traveling by plane, again departed for foreign lands and more consultations. In a hotel just outside Cairo, Egypt, he met both Prime Minister Churchill and Generalissimo Chiang Kai-shek. For four days, November 22-26, these three men, representing the United States, Great Britain and China, respectively, talked together as to how they could best unite in conquering Japan, a country which China had been fighting for weary years before America entered the war. A communiqué, issued after the conference had ended, declared:

> "The three great powers, the United States, Great Britain, and China, had reached full agreement to press unrelenting war against their brutal enemies by land, sea and air; to renounce all territorial gains for themselves and to strip the Japanese of all Pacific islands seized since 1914; to restore to China the lost lands of Manchuria, Formosa and the Pescadores; to expel Japan from all territory she had taken by violence and greed; to guarantee the future independence of enslaved Korea; and to persevere in the serious and prolonged operations necessary to procure the unconditional surrender of Japan."

After leaving Cairo, President Roosevelt and Prime Minister Churchill went to Teheran, the capital of

"The Big Three"—Prime Minister Winston Churchill, President Roosevelt and Marshal Stalin—met at Teheran and again at Yalta to discuss international affairs. Behind them stand the three Foreign Secretaries: Anthony Eden, Great Britain; Edward Stettinius, United States; and Molotoff, Russia.

Iran (once known as Persia), to meet Marshal Stalin of Russia. It was the first time that Mr. Roosevelt had met Marshal Stalin. It was said to be the first time that Marshal Stalin had left the Soviet Union since the revolution of 1917. Mr. Churchill stayed at the British Embassy.

This was a dramatic meeting among the three world leaders. At its close the three men issued a proclamation expressing "our determination that our nations shall work together in the war and in the peace that will follow," stating that final plans had been made for the destruction of the German forces, and asserting confidence in "an enduring peace."

After Teheran, Mr. Roosevelt and Mr. Churchill met still another ruler. They conferred with President Ismet Inonu of Turkey. These three issued a declaration that "the closest unity existed between the United States of America, Turkey and Great Britain in their attitude toward the world situation." But no change resulted in the Turkish foreign policy. Turkey remained neutral.

President Roosevelt returned to the United States on December 16th, having traveled an estimated distance of 25,000 miles since his departure on November 11th. He stated publicly that the conference had been a success in every way. In a Christmas Eve broadcast, he said the four powers—the United States, Great Britain, China and Russia—had agreed to use force to maintain peace after victory.

CHAPTER TWENTY

A FOURTH TERM

The year 1944 was an election year. The people were anxious to find out if Mr. Roosevelt would run again. There was much public discussion as to whether he would or would not be a candidate for a fourth term. Early in the summer Mr. Roosevelt set discussion and speculation at rest. He wrote Democratic National Chairman Hannegan that, though he wanted to retire, yet "If the convention should nominate me for the presidency, I shall accept." He further wrote Mr. Hannegan that he—Mr. Roosevelt—would not run in the ordinary political sense of getting out and waging an active campaign. "But," said Mr. Roosevelt, "if the people command me to continue in this office and in this war, I have as little right to withdraw as the soldier has to leave his post in the line."

The national Democratic convention was held in Chicago in July. Mr. Roosevelt easily won the nomination for the Presidency. The man chosen to run for the Vice-Presidency was Senator Harry Truman, a junior senator from Missouri.

In his speech of acceptance, delivered the night following his nomination and made from his private railroad car on the West coast, Mr. Roosevelt said, "I shall not campaign in the usual sense for the office. In these days of tragic sorrow, I do not consider it fitting. And, besides, in these days of global warfare I shall not be able to find the time. The people of the United States will decide this Fall whether they wish to turn over this 1944 job, this world-wide job, to inexperienced or immature hands."

The Republican party chose as its candidate for the presidency Governor Thomas E. Dewey, a young man who was governor of New York state. Thus the youngest candidate in history—Governor Dewey—was running against one of the oldest—President Roosevelt—but who was also a very astute politician.

Absorbed in matters pertaining to the war, Mr. Roosevelt did very little real campaigning. In October he took time for one trip through several states, making speeches from the rear platform of his train and in a few cities, including Philadelphia and New York. He headed a parade in New York City. Rain fell in torrents throughout the day. In spite of it, large crowds filled the streets to glimpse Mr. Roosevelt. The top of the presidential car was down. Wrapped in his old Navy cape, the President took the downpour throughout the entire parade, as he had following his second inauguration. Most of the time he smiled his famous radiant smile. At other times he relaxed and the reporters said he looked tired. His appearance in the rain contradicted rumors that his health was failing; and perhaps he appeared for that very reason.

On election day Mr. Roosevelt voted, as was his custom, at Hyde Park. At the polls he gave his occupation as "tree grower." That night he, his family and his secretaries kept the election returns as they came in.

It soon became apparent that he had won. The usual torchlight parade of neighbors marched up the driveway to Hyde Park House to congratulate him. Mr. Roosevelt was wheeled out on the piazza and made a very happy speech. He recalled that he had seen his first torchlight parade from the village when Grover Cleveland was elected and he, a youngster, got out of bed to witness it.

Mr. Roosevelt had been elected for a fourth term largely because a majority of the voters believed that he was indispensable to winning the war and they thought it would be unwise to risk changing Presidents in wartime. This same majority of voters also believed Mr. Roosevelt was the one American qualified to deal successfully with the leaders of other nations, particularly with Prime Minister Churchill and Marshal Stalin. The people of other nations also had faith in him. They believed Mr. Roosevelt could make a just and lasting peace. The whole world had followed the election returns.

Senator Harry Truman was elected Vice-President. No one could look into the future and see that before many months Mr. Truman was to become President.

Throughout 1944 and the early part of 1945, American and Allied forces won victory after victory in both Europe and the Pacific area. Seeing that World War II was fast approaching its end, Mr. Roosevelt began to work out plans to prevent a third world war. He hoped to do this through nations working together. He wanted to create a world organization to maintain peace and security. It was to replace the League of Nations and avoid the mistakes which kept the United States out of the League.

This nation was at war; therefore, elaborate inauguration ceremonies seemed out of place. Mr. Roosevelt's fourth inauguration as President was the simplest of all. It took place on the back porch of the White House. Snow had fallen the night before, turning to sleet, so that Washington was an all white city. Before the inauguration, Mr. Roosevelt, with two hundred and fifty close friends and members of his official family, attended divine services in the East Room instead of going to St. John's Episcopal Church, as had been Mr. Roosevelt's custom before his other inaugurations. He joined in singing the hymn, "O, God, Our Help in Ages Past." The prayers were for peace.

Later in the morning the crowd of 8,000 guests, wearing warm coats and galoshes, gathered on the snowy lawn below the south portico. On the south portico, above the crowd, were Supreme Court Justices, Cabinet members, close friends and their wives, the immediate Roosevelt family, including the President's thirteen grandchildren. Promptly at noon, the Marine Band burst into "Hail to the Chief." The Right Reverend Dunn, Episcopal Bishop of Washington, offered the prayer.

Mr. Roosevelt was grave, as befitting the leader of a nation at war. His eyes were lifted above the crowd to the Washington Monument and the Jefferson Memorial in the background. He placed his right hand on the same old family Bible, on the same page, where he had placed it at five previous inaugurations (two as

The fourth inauguration of President Roosevelt. Harry Truman, left, had just been inaugurated as Vice-President, later becoming President upon Roosevelt's death. James Roosevelt, President Roosevelt's oldest son, right, is saluting.

Governor of New York, three as President) , the thirteenth chapter of First Corinthians, which ends: *And
now abideth faith, hope, charity, these three: but the
greatest of these is charity.* His voice was clear as he re-
peated the oath after Chief Justice Stone, ending with
so help me God. He then delivered the shortest inaugural speech that he had ever made. In it he expressed the
hope that the United States would abandon its tradi-
tional policy of isolation and join with other Allied
nations in the formation of an international organization to maintain peace after victory. He made no men-
tion of domestic affairs. He mentioned war very little.
His thoughts were on the kind of a world that would
follow the peace. He said:

"In the days and years that are to come we shall work
for a just and honorable peace, a durable peace. . . . We
shall strive for perfection. We shall not achieve it immediately—but we shall strive.

"We have learned lessons—at a fearful cost—and we
shall profit by them. We have learned that we can not
live alone, at peace. We have learned that we must live
as men, and not as ostriches, nor as dogs in the manger.
We have learned the simple truth, as Emerson said,
that 'the only way to have a friend is to be one.' "

The President went inside. So did the 2,000 friends
who were invited to luncheon—a "wartime" luncheon
consisting of chicken salad, hard rolls without butter,
cake without icing, and coffee. Many other guests came
to tea that afternoon.

A few days after his fourth inauguration, Mr. Roosevelt left Washington on a Navy warship for another—

and it was to be his last—foreign conference in the Crimea. With him were Secretary of State Edward Stettinius, Harry Hopkins, James F. Byrnes, and a host of government and military leaders, including General Marshall, Admirals King and Leahy. In addition to this staff of advisers and officials went his daughter Anna, Mrs. John Boettiger. During this trip, as at the White House, Mrs. Boettiger watched over her father's health and kept him constant company. When he had important guests for lunch—Prime Minister Churchill, General Marshall, Admiral King—Mrs. Boettiger was hostess.

Mr. Roosevelt reached Malta, the first stop on the trip to the Crimea, on February 2nd. Prime Minister Churchill was there to greet him. Mr. Roosevelt and Mrs. Boettiger entertained Prime Minister Churchill and his daughter, Sarah Churchill, aboard a United States cruiser.

After a day of conferences at Malta, Mr. Roosevelt and his party boarded planes to take them to the Crimea. Near Yalta, in what had been a summer estate of the czars of Russia, they were joined by Marshal Stalin. Mr. Roosevelt occupied a suite in a palace that was built of white marble and contained about fifty rooms. It appeared very vast and imposing after the small size and simplicity of the White House, the home of the Presidents of the United States.

The overall problems were threshed out by the "big three"—President Roosevelt, Prime Minister Churchill and Marshal Stalin; international problems by the diplomats; and military problems by the officers of the

Army and Navy. The Crimean declaration reaffirmed the pledge of the Atlantic Charter for a free world. The "big three" decided that they had agreed on the terms of surrender for Germany and on a method of occupation afterward. It was decided at Yalta to call a United Nations Security Organization on April 25th, 1945, to be held at San Francisco. President Roosevelt was to open it.

After leaving Yalta, Mr. Roosevelt had more interviews with foreign rulers, who visited him on the U. S. cruiser. Among them were King Farouk, of Egypt; Ibn Saud, King of Saudi Arabia; Emperor Haile Selassie. King Ibn Saud spent the night on a U. S. destroyer, bringing with him thick Oriental rugs and a royal tent that was pitched on deck and in which he slept. With him were his brother, two sons, many bodyguards and representatives of native tribes. He also brought his own food, including a flock of sheep, for which a pen had to be built on the destroyer's deck. The surroundings were almost those of a fairy tale.

Immediately upon his return from the Crimea, President Roosevelt addressed Congress to tell the members about the conferences in which he had taken part while he was away. In spite of his difficulty in walking, the President had heretofore always stood when he spoke to Congress. On this occasion, for the first time he sat in a wheel chair while he spoke. He explained that he preferred to sit rather than stand because he did not want to be burdened with "ten pounds of steel braces," referring to the heavy braces on his legs that enabled him to stand and to walk. He began his speech by saying, "It is good to be home. It has been a long journey. I hope you will agree that it has been a fruitful one." He seemed gay and confident, and contradicted rumors that he had been ill by saying, "I am returning refreshed and inspired. I was well the entire time." In spite of this statement, photographs showed him looking worn and tired. The reporters present reported that he was tanned from his trip but gray and thin. Referring to his trip, he said, "The Roosevelts are not, as you may well suspect, averse to travel."

The theme of his message to Congress was: "We shall have to take the responsibility for world collaboration or we shall have to bear the responsibility for another world conflict." The newspapers said that the Crimean conference was the most famous of Mr. Roosevelt's series of conferences with Prime Minister Churchill and Marshal Stalin.

After this return, Mr. Roosevelt's time was devoted largely to plans for future world peace after victory over Germany. According to confidential military information furnished him, he knew that victory would come reasonably soon. He prepared particularly for the World Security Conference to be held at San Francisco in April.

On March 30th he went to Warm Springs, Georgia, for a rest of several weeks. "My second home," he called Warm Springs, and this was his second visit there within four months. He had gone there first in the summer of 1924; he had bought a farm there. Because he loved Warm Springs, he seemed to relax more there than anywhere else. Swimming in the warm waters of the pool also helped his paralyzed legs.

At the end of his rest he expected to return to Washington for one day before leaving for San Francisco to open the United Nations conference. Though he was worn by the war and underweight, and had been sent by his doctors to Warm Springs to try to regain those lost pounds, no danger to his health was feared. This was shown by the fact that no member of his family, not even his wife or his daughter Anna, went with him. Neither was there any close friend nor his personal physician, Admiral Ross McIntyre. Accompanying him was Commander Howard Bruenen, a Naval doctor, who looked after Mr. Roosevelt's health at Warm Springs.

CHAPTER TWENTY-ONE

A SOLDIER DIES

"I have a terrific headache," said President Roosevelt suddenly one day.

It was Thursday, April 12th, 1945. Mr. Roosevelt sat in front of the fireplace in the living room of his cottage, often called the Little White House, at Warm Springs. He appeared in the best of spirits on that mild spring day. A woman artist was sketching him while he signed important papers sent from Washington; she said afterward that he was so gay. "Here is where I make a law," he had remarked, as he often did when signing important papers that created laws. He continued to sign his name.

Without warning, he said that his head ached terrifically. Those were his last words. He fell over in his chair in what seemed to be a faint and, without regaining consciousness, died two hours later from a severe cerebral, or brain, hemorrhage. His age was sixty-three years.

His totally unexpected death was soon spread by radio. It came as a thunderbolt to the entire world. The only president to be elected for more than two terms, he had held office a little more than twelve years, more than four years longer than any other president. He had become a recognized leader in world affairs as well as in those at home. New need for his vigorous leadership lay ahead in assuring world peace. And now he was gone, his death due to overwork caused by the war, so that he was as much a battle casualty as any soldier who died in combat.

Nowhere was the news a greater shock than at Warm Springs. Since his arrival, he had driven around constantly, as was his custom, taking long rides over the pine-forested hills in the spring sunshine. He had shown his usual enthusiastic interest in local matters. That evening the polio patients at the Infantile Paralysis Foundation were giving a minstrel show for him. That fatal afternoon he was expected to attend a barbecue in his honor. Mayor Frank Alcorn, host for the barbecue, and about fifty friends were awaiting the President's arrival when they were stunned to hear of his death.

The sad news reached the White House at once. Mrs. Roosevelt was attending a tea for the benefit of the children's clinics of Washington. Secretary Steve Early phoned her and asked her to hurry to the White House. He then told her of this great sorrow that had come to her, to her children, to the United States, and to the world. He said, "The President has slept away."

Mrs. Roosevelt immediately sent a message to her four sons in service. After telling them that their father had passed away, she said, "He did his job to the end as he would want you to do. Bless you and all our love. Mother."

As soon as she had rallied from the first great shock, Mrs. Roosevelt began thinking of others and of what Mr. Roosevelt's death meant in world terms. She said to Secretary Early and Admiral McIntyre, "I am more sorry for the people of the country and the world than I am for us."

Vice-President Truman, at the Capitol, also received an urgent message to come to the White House. Mrs. Roosevelt herself told him of the President's death. He inquired what he could do for her and she replied, "Tell us what we can do. Is there anything we can do for you?"

In order that the United States should not be without a President, Vice-President Truman was immediately sworn in as the President of the United States. He took the oath of office, administered by Chief Justice Harlan P. Stone, in the Cabinet room of the White House, surrounded by his wife and daughter and the members of the former President's Cabinet. It was only 82 days since Justice Stone had, on the rear portico of the White House, sworn in Franklin Delano Roosevelt for a fourth term. Now the Chief Justice was swearing in a new President.

After dark, Mrs. Roosevelt left by plane for Warm Springs to accompany the body of the late President back to Washington. With her went Rear Admiral McIntyre, Navy surgeon general and White House physician.

On Friday morning an impressive funeral procession left the little cottage on Pine Mountain, in Warm Springs. Honoring their late commander-in-chief, a band of the 99th Army Ground Forces from Fort Benning, Georgia, led the procession. Two battalions of troops (infantry and paratroops) stood at attention along the red dirt road and the highway leading from the 2,000-acre grounds of the Warm Springs Infantile Paralysis Foundation to the village railroad station where Mr. Roosevelt had often arrived. Eight bearers—four soldiers and two each from the Navy and Marines—carried the mahogany casket from the cottage through a portico over which red roses climbed. Behind the hearse came Mrs. Roosevelt, dressed in black; at her feet in the car sat Fala, a bewildered little dog who could not understand why he had lost the big, laughing master he loved.

The procession stopped for a moment before the main building of the Infantile Paralysis Foundation. All the patients who could leave their beds were out in front on crutches and in wheel chairs, tiny tots to middle-aged men and women, some in Army and Navy uniforms. Tears poured down many of their faces. They were there to say goodbye to the man who had made the place, with its cures, possible for them. During the brief stop a Negro musician, who had often played for the President, played *Going Home* softly on an accordion.

As the funeral train sped north, silent, sad-faced crowds, white and Negro, stood at every station along the route. They represented people mourning everywhere for the man who had led America almost to victory and to whom they looked for assuring world peace after the war was won.

The train reached Washington on Saturday morning. Members of the Roosevelt family, President Truman and his wife, high-ranking officials and diplomats,

The funeral procession, more than a mile long, passed slowly along Pennsylvania Avenue. As many as 500,000 people watched Franklin D. Roosevelt ride down the Avenue once more.

some of whom had often come to welcome Franklin Delano Roosevelt back from his many trips, were at the Union Station for his last arrival. Mrs. Boettiger was the first to enter the funeral car.

The procession, more than a mile long, passed slowly along Pennsylvania Avenue to the White House. Two bands, one Marine and the other Naval, played solemn music. The coffin, covered by a United States flag, was borne on a black gun caisson drawn by six white horses. With the casket came marching troops—armored troops, infantry, cadets, Marines, Waves, Wacs and Spars. Immense crowds, silent and sorrowful, jammed the sidewalks. As many as 500,000 people, who had often watched Mr. Roosevelt on his inaugurations and many other notable occasions as he had ridden down this Avenue, now watched him ride down it once more.

Arriving at the White House, the coffin was placed in the East Room. An American flag stood on one side and the President's own flag on the other. A sailor, a flier, a Marine and a soldier, in uniform and under a young lieutenant, representing the Armed Forces, stood guard near the four corners of the casket.

At four o'clock the funeral service was held in the East Room, its walls almost covered with flowers though the family had requested that none be sent. Only about two hundred people could be seated in the East Room, so only the family, close friends, high officials and diplomats could be invited. Other mourners and employees spread out into the Blue and Green Rooms. Though necessarily small in number, those present included many distinguished people. President and

Mrs. Truman sat in the front row in the East Room. Anthony Eden, representing Prime Minister Churchill, was there; Mr. Eden had flown across the Atlantic Ocean to be present. Bernard Baruch, known as an "elder statesman," an old and valued friend who had been in England on a special mission for the President, had also flown across the ocean to attend the funeral. Brigadier General Elliott Roosevelt, the only one of the Roosevelt sons who could get home, had come across the ocean too. The Earl of Athlone, Governor General of Canada and uncle of King George, represented the British royal family. Near the Roosevelts sat Harry Hopkins, the President's intimate friend, who had gone to all the "big three" conferences with Mr. Roosevelt; Mr. Hopkins had come from a hospital, where he had been ill, to honor the man he loved devotedly. The President's empty wheel chair stood in front.

The service was impressive and very short. Lasting only twenty-five minutes, it lacked pomp and eulogies, as if the useful and courageous life of Franklin Delano Roosevelt spoke for itself without words of praise. It was conducted by Bishop Angus Dunn. The hymns sung, both favorites of Mr. Roosevlt, were *Eternal Father Strong to Serve* and *Faith of Our Fathers,* in which those present joined. Stenographers and clerks of the White House offices, gathered in the lobby of the adjoining office building, listened to the service through a loud speaker.

Bishop Dunn said, "In his first inaugural address, the President bore testimony to his own deep faith;

so, first of all, let me assert my own belief that 'the only thing we have to fear is fear itself'."

In his final prayer Bishop Dunn prayed, "O God, from Whom every good gift cometh, we thank Thee for the qualities of heart and mind which this Thy servant brought to the service of our nation and our world.

"For steadfast courage in adversity, for clear visions of dangers to which they may shut their eyes; for sympathy with the hungers and fears of common men; for trials met without surrender, and weakness endured without defeat; for unyielding faith in the possibility of a more just and ordered world, delivered from the ancient curse of war; we praise Thee, O God."

At the funeral hour the entire nation paid tribute to the late President. War industries paused. Stores and government offices closed. Individuals stood still to pray. The Armed Forces over the world, when not engaged in combat, paused five minutes for silent prayer. The bell of St. John's Episcopal Church, across Pennsylvania Avenue from the White House, tolled in mourning during the funeral.

That night the funeral party boarded a special train for Hyde Park. Franklin Roosevelt really went home then, to the spot he loved best, where he had spent his childhood and his happiest hours; where he went to rest in later years from heavy burdens and responsibilities that came to him with high place; where he voted; where he planted trees and drove his own car over his own roads; where he had entertained the King and the Queen of England and other high personages.

Here he was buried on Sunday morning in a quiet
rose garden in the spot he had chosen for his resting
place.

The group at the grave included friends, relatives,
the new President of the United States, ambassadors,
old neighbors, the secretaries. A squad of West Point
cadets fired several volleys. A bugle sounded taps. The
funeral ended at 10:45.

After the crowd had left, Mrs. Roosevelt came back
to stand alone, a silent, solitary figure, watching the
workmen shovel soil into her husband's grave.

Though Franklin Roosevelt had died physically, he
has continued to live in the hearts of his fellow men
because of what he tried to do for human beings. He
loved people. Through this love of them, he had an
immense understanding of their problems and their
needs. Bishop Oxnam, of the Methodist church, said
of him, "President Franklin Roosevelt honestly believed that ideals should be translated into the practices
of the common life. . . . He loved the common man,
he labored to enrich the lives of the people."

CHAPTER TWENTY-TWO

THE MAN HE WAS

Many Americans felt Mr. Roosevelt's death as a personal sorrow. "It's almost like losing a member of my family," they said. He was mourned not only by the people of the United States but all over the world. It was said that the English mourned him as if he had been their king. In the opinion of foreigners, he was a very great man.

Our soldiers, both officers and privates, missed him particularly. They were young men, and Mr. Roosevelt had been President a large part of their lives. He was also their commander-in-chief. They were proud of his prestige abroad, of his ability to deal with Prime Minister Churchill and Marshal Stalin.

"I can remember the President ever since I was a kid," said one GI. "America will seem a strange, empty place without his voice talking to the people when great events occur."

It was indeed hard to think that Franklin Delano Roosevelt had gone. He had been a man so vitally alive, so full of tremendous energy—despite his inability to walk unaided after he was stricken with infantile paralysis. Handsome, he had a distinguished bearing. Possessing unusual personal charm, he owned in a rare degree that elusive quality admired especially by young people. His famous smile radiated good cheer and deep interest in people and their problems. His wonderful speaking voice, deep, rich, mellow—"the voice with a smile," someone called it—had been carried by radio into American homes so that it was instantly recognized by any listener. When the hour arrived for one of his fireside chats, and Mr. Roosevelt began, "My Friends," Americans pulled their chairs near the radio and listened intently, as if he and they were in reality sitting together around an actual fireside and talking over the problems of the times in which they were both deeply interested.

Perhaps his strongest trait, both personally and politically, was his absolute lack of fear. Said a young congressman about Mr. Roosevelt at the time of his death, "He was the only person I have ever known—anywhere —who was not afraid." Everyone remembers his dramatic utterance at the time of his first inauguration, "The only thing we have to fear is fear itself." He exemplified this trait in his lack of fear of infantile paralysis and his gallant conquest of that dread disease. He showed it in the summer of 1915 when, as Assistant-Secretary of the Navy, he insisted on going down in a submarine off the West Coast after one had just been sunk with everyone on board. He evidenced it time after time during his entire life.

Another equally strong trait was self-confidence. It probably sprang from his total lack of fear. Self-confidence prompted him, when he had determined on a course of action, to go ahead with it regardless of what others thought or advised. People who disliked him—and there were plenty of them—said this trait was just plain stubbornness inherited from his Dutch ancestors. People who admired him called him "a great-hearted fighter." Undoubtedly, he relished a good fight and never went out of his way to avoid one. He usually fought for underprivileged people and for small nations but it was said that he never lost his temper in a fight.

Leadership was a third trait. Franklin Roosevelt had always been a leader in any group with which he became associated, from the playmates of his childhood on through political life until he became not only a national leader but a world leader as well. Through his leadership in his later years he exerted a tremendous influence on the United States and the entire world. It was said at the time of his death that he had done more to mold the United States and the world he lived in than anyone else. A man who is a leader pays a price. He is bound to antagonize the people he opposes and the causes he fights. This was true of Franklin Roosevelt. His quality of leadership caused him to be both loved and hated equally by great numbers of people. He had in an amazing degree the loyalty and affection of countless millions as well as the strong dislike of other millions.

Will power was an extremely strong trait, or perhaps it developed as his need for it arose. Only a person possessing tremendous will power could have forced himself, as Mr. Roosevelt did, to undergo the slow and tedious exercises that were necessary for a long time, before any improvement, even the slightest, could be felt in the condition of his legs. He never spared

himself because of his physical handicap. Though
walking and standing undoubtedly required tremendous physical effort on his part, yet he made his gallant,
crippled body do these things (walk and stand) as
if they were not hard; therefore, few people watching
him dreamed of the determination it took to perform
such seemingly simple acts.

There were other traits. All of them combined to
form a remarkably well-rounded person who left his
impress on the majority of those who knew him.

He had a gift for expressing himself in vivid phrases
that stuck in the mind of the public. In accepting his
first nomination for the Presidency at the Democratic
National Convention in Chicago, on July 2, 1932, he
pledged himself to "a new deal for the American
people." Henceforth, through four Presidential campaigns and many stirring legislative battles, the term
New Deal stood for the domestic policies he favored.
In the field of foreign relations, he coined an almost
equally well-known phrase. In his first inaugural address he declared he would dedicate the United States
to the policy of "the good neighbor." In his efforts
to improve the living conditions of the poor, he said
that "one-third of this nation is . . . ill-fed, ill-clothed
and ill-housed." Such sayings as these have become a
part of our American vocabulary.

His death came at an hour of great triumph. The
armies and fleets under him as commander-in-chief
were on the verge of victory over Germany and Japan.
If he had lived, his leadership would have been turned
from the problems of war toward the problems of a

coming peace. The night before he died, he wrote a speech to be delivered at numerous Jefferson Day dinners to be held all over the country on the following Friday night. After his death this speech was given to the press. It showed his strong desire for world peace. In it he said, "We seek peace, enduring peace. More than an end to war, we want an end to the beginnings of all war."

When he died so suddenly that the world was stunned by the news, there were many public expressions of regret from important people over his death. Only a few of these opinions are quoted. Even the men who had opposed him conceded the severity of the loss sustained by his death. The statement of Senator Taft, a Republican who differed constantly with Mr. Roosevelt on policy, is typical of many others. Said Senator Taft, "The greatest figure in our time has been removed at the very climax of his career. He died a hero of the war, for he literally worked himself to death in the service of the American people."

Governor Thomas Dewey of New York State, who as the Republican candidate for the Presidency had been defeated by Mr. Roosevelt the previous year, said, "With a deep sense of tragedy the nation learns of the loss of Franklin Delano Roosevelt, one of the great Presidents of the United States. Coming to leadership of the nation at a critical period in our economic life, he brought high courage and indomitable spirit to the task of meeting the most difficult of national problems, inspiring the people with fresh confidence and establishing basic liberal reforms. Every American, of every shade of opinion, will mourn the loss of Franklin Roosevelt as a human being of warm human qualities and great capacities."

Mayor LaGuardia of New York City: "It is the greatest loss the peace-loving people of the world have suffered in the entire war. The shock is so great that it is extremely difficult for one to realize what has happened. There is only one thing we can do as good Americans—to pay adequate tribute to this war casualty—and that is to unite in carrying out his ideals for world justice and human peace."

James M. Cox, Democratic nominee for the Presidency in 1920 with whom Mr. Roosevelt ran—and lost —for the Vice-Presidency: "The saddest thing of all is that death had to deny to the President the hour of what would have been his two greatest triumphs— victory to our arms and lasting peace for the peoples of the earth. He was so much a part of both and carried them so near to completion that history will ascribe them largely to his genius and humanity."

Dr. James B. Conant, President of Harvard: "The sudden death of President Roosevelt at this moment in our history is a world tragedy of such magnitude as to render trivial all conventional expressions of grief and homage. Friends of freedom in all countries must respond to this challenge given them by fate and insure by their efforts the realization of his aims."

Prime Minister John Curtin of Australia: "This is a sad day for the United States; it is a sad day for the world. When the British race had the honor of standing alone against the aggressor, it was this man who guided

his people toward the purpose he always had upper-
most in mind. Australia will not forget him for his
sympathy, understanding and great help in the dark
days of our trial. His memory will be ever green in
the minds of Australians."

Queen Wilhelmina and Princess Juliana of the
Netherlands: "He gave his life for our common cause
and the Netherlands will ever cherish his name."

The newspapers and magazines were filled with
opinions of him. The New York *Times* said editorially:

> . "Gone is the exuberance and the enthusiasm and
> the indomitable courage that conquered the hardest
> of personal afflictions and the worst handicap of
> physical misfortune. Gone is the fresh and sponta-
> neous interest which this man took, as naturally as he
> breathed air, in the troubles and the hardships and
> the disappointments and the hopes of little men and
> humble people.
>
> "The central issue of this war has been the very
> life or death of the civilization we have built.
>
> "This man, taxing the strength of a crippled body
> to its limit, in the noblest cause of modern times,
> died as a soldier in the line of duty.
>
> "He fought with deep convictions and unmeasured
> devotion for what he believed to be the common
> rights of all men.
>
> "After his vigorous conduct of the war, it seemed
> a bitter irony that he did not live to see the Allied
> armies march into Berlin."

On the first anniversary of Mr. Roosevelt's death,
Hyde Park House, in Dutchess County, New York,
where the Roosevelts had lived for many years, became
a historic national shrine. The official ceremonies were

On the first anniversary of President Roosevelt's death, Hyde Park House, through its gift to the nation by the Roosevelt family, became a national shrine. Mrs. Roosevelt and President Truman lead the procession.

held on the broad front porch where Mr. Roosevelt had so often cordially welcomed visitors and especially his neighbors on election nights. Mrs. Eleanor Roosevelt turned over the large residence and about thirty-three acres of land to the people of the United States. In presenting this generous gift from herself and her children, Mrs. Roosevelt said:

"This is the house where my husband was born and brought up. He loved this house. Here he played as a child. Here he spent the summer, nine months after he was stricken. Here he grew strong. So it is with no regret that I see this house and its contents dedicated to the people whom my husband loved."

President Truman accepted the gift on behalf of the government. In his speech of acceptance he pledged his administration to carry forward the underlying principles and policies, foreign and domestic, of Franklin Roosevelt.

Thousands of people will visit Hyde Park House in the years to come. They will find the inside arranged the way it was the last time Mr. Roosevelt left it. They may study the bird collection he made as a boy. They will see Mr. Roosevelt's bedroom, its windows giving a wide view of the Hudson River, his wheelchair standing beside his bed, and his clothes, including his favorite old Navy cape, hanging in the closet. In the large library they may examine the maps on which he followed the war.

Before leaving Hyde Park, visitors will want to go to the rose garden and stand in reverent silence beside Mr. Roosevelt's grave. It is marked by a simple white stone, according to a memorandum he made in 1937, that "a plain white monument is to be placed over my grave." May those who stand beside the grave remember that Franklin Roosevelt is the man who called for a future world founded on the four freedoms as the essential right of every human being, everywhere.

In the hours before dawn of July 6th, 1944, as he lay awake in his bed in the White House awaiting the news of the invasion of Normandy, in which he knew that the lives of many American boys would be given for the cause of freedom, Mr. Roosevelt wrote a prayer. All of it is indicative of his spirit. The latter part, about the brotherhood of man, should remain with each person who wants to do his share toward a better world which Franklin Roosevelt tried to create.

"Yet, most of all, grant us brotherhood, not only for this day but for all our years, a brotherhood not of words but of acts and deeds. We are all of us children of earth—grant us that simple knowledge. If our brothers are oppressed, then we are oppressed. If they hunger, we hunger. If their freedom is taken away, our freedom is not secure. Grant us a common faith that man shall know bread and peace, that he shall know justice and righteousness, freedom and security, an equal opportunity and an equal chance to do his best, not only in our own lands but throughout the world, and in that faith let us march toward the clean world our hands can make."

God grant that his prayer come true.

CHAPTER TWENTY-THREE

EXTRACTS FROM PUBLIC SPEECHES

SPIRITUAL VALUES

The people of the United States still recognize, and I believe, recognize with a firmer faith than ever before, that spiritual values count in the long run more than material values. Those people in other lands who have sought by edict or by law to eliminate the right of mankind to believe in God and to practice that belief, have, in every known case, discovered sooner or later that they are tilting in vain against an inherent, essential, underlying quality, indeed necessity, of the human race—a quality and a necessity which in every century have proved an essential to permanent progress—and I speak of religion.

The spirit of America springs from faith—faith in the beloved institutions of our land, and a true and abiding faith in the divine guidance of God.

New York, 1933

THE GOOD NEIGHBOR

In the field of world policy, I would dedicate this nation to the policy of the good neighbor—the neighbor who resolutely respects himself and, because he does so, respects the rights of others—the neighbor who

167

respects his obligations and respects the sanctity of his agreements in and with a world of neighbors.

First Inaugural Address, 1933

MEANING OF LIBERTY

I am not for a return to that definition of liberty under which for many years a free people were being gradually regimented into the service of the privileged few. I prefer and I am sure you prefer that broader definition of liberty under which we are moving forward to greater freedom, to greater security for the average man than he has ever known before in the history of America.

Fireside Chat, 1934

COST OF DICTATORSHIP

Dictatorship involves costs which the American people will never pay: The cost of our spiritual values. The cost of the blessed right of being able to say what we please. The cost of freedom of religion. The cost of seeing our capital confiscated. The cost of being cast into a concentration camp. The cost of being afraid to walk down the street with the wrong neighbor. The cost of having our children brought up, not as free and dignified human beings, but as pawns molded and enslaved by a machine.

Message to Congress, 1939

NOT FOR HOMES ALONE

There comes a time in the affairs of men when they must prepare to defend, not their homes alone, but the tenets of faith and humanity on which their churches, their governments and their very civilization are founded. The defense of religion, of democracy and of good faith among nations is all the same fight. To save one we must now make up our minds to save all.

The world has grown so small and weapons of attack so swift that no nation can be safe in its will to peace so long as any other powerful nation refuses to settle its grievances at the council table.

We have learned that God-fearing democracies of the world which observe the sanctities of treaties and good faith in their dealings with other nations can not safely be indifferent to international lawlessness anywhere. They can not forever let pass, without effective protest, acts of aggression against sister nations —acts which automatically undermine all of us.

Message to Congress, 1939

THE WEAK AND THE STRONG

We are a nation of many nationalities, many races, many religions—bound together by a single unity, the unity of freedom and equality. Whoever seeks to set one nationality against another seeks to degrade all nationalities. Whoever seeks to set one race against another seeks to enslave all races. Whoever seeks to set one religion against another seeks to destroy all religion. I am fighting for a free America—for a country in which *all* men and women have equal rights to liberty and justice. I am fighting, as I have always fought, for the rights of the little man as well as the big man—for the weak as well as the strong, for those who are helpless as well as those who can help themselves.

Talk to the Nation, 1940

THE COMMON PEOPLE

Democracy can thrive only when it enlists the devotion of those whom Lincoln called the common people. Democracy can hold that devotion only when it adequately respects their dignity by so ordering society as to assure to the masses of men and women reasonable security and hope for themselves and their children.

Talk to the Nation, 1940

THE FOUR FREEDOMS

In the future days, which we seek to make secure, we look forward to a world founded upon four essential human freedoms.

The first is freedom of speech and expression—everywhere in the world.

The second is freedom of every person to worship God in his own way—everywhere in the world.

The third is freedom from want—which, translated into world terms, means economic understandings which will secure to every nation a healthy peacetime life for its inhabitants—everywhere in the world.

The fourth is freedom from fear—which, translated into world terms, means a world-wide reduction of armaments to such a point and in such a thorough fashion that no nation will be in a position to commit an act of physical aggression against any neighbor —anywhere in the world.

Message to Congress, 1941

DIVIDED YET UNITED

The dictators can not seem to realize that here in America our people can maintain two parties and at the same time maintain an inviolate and indivisible nation. The totalitarian mentality is too narrow to comprehend the greatness of a people who can be divided in party allegiance at election time, yet remain united in devotion to their country and to the ideals of democracy at all times.

In our country, disagreements among us are expressed at the polling place. In the dictatorships, disagreements are expressed in the concentration camp.

Talk to the Nation, 1941

CHOICE BETWEEN HITLER'S WORLD AND OURS

All of us Americans, of all opinions, are faced with the choice between the kind of a world we want to live in and the kind of a world which Hitler and his hordes would impose on us. None of us wants to burrow under the ground and live in total darkness like a comfortable mole.

Very simply and very bluntly we are pledged to pull our own oar in the destruction of Hitlerism.

And when we have helped to end the curse of Hitlerism, we shall help to establish a new peace which will give to decent people everywhere a better chance to live and prosper in security and in freedom and in faith.

Talk to the Nation, 1941

There is no such thing as security for any nation—or any individual—in a world ruled by the principles of gangsterism. There is no such thing as impregnable defense against powerful aggressors who sneak up in the dark and strike without warning. We have learned that our ocean-girt hemisphere is not immune from severe attack—that we can not measure our safety in terms of miles on any map.

We may acknowledge that our enemies have performed a brilliant feat of deception, perfectly timed and executed with great skill. It was a thoroughly dishonorable deed, but we must face the fact that modern warfare as conducted in the Nazi manner is a dirty business. We don't like it—we didn't want to get in it— but we are in it and we're going to fight it with everything we've got.

We are going to win the war, and we are going to win the peace that follows. And in the dark hours of this day—and through dark days that may be yet to come— we will know that the vast majority of the members of the human race are on our side. Many of them are fighting with us. All of them are praying for us. For, in representing our cause, we represent theirs as well— our hope and their hope for liberty under God.

Talk to the Nation, December 8, 1941
(Night following Pearl Harbor attack.)

OUR GOAL

It would be inconceivable—it would, indeed, be sacrilegious—if this nation and the world did not attain some real, lasting good out of all these efforts and sufferings and bloodshed and death. The men in our armed forces want a lasting peace and, equally, they want permanent employment for themselves, their families and their neighbors when they are mustered out at the end of the war.

We fight to retain a great past—and we fight to gain a greater future. Today the United Nations are the mightiest coalition in history. They can and must remain united for the maintenance of the peace by preventing any attempt to rearm in Germany, in Japan, in Italy, or in any other nation that seeks to violate the Tenth Commandment—"Thou shalt not covet."

Message to Congress, 1943

ECONOMIC BILL OF RIGHTS

We have accepted, so to speak, a second bill of rights under which a new basis of security and prosperity can be established for all, regardless of station, race or creed. Among these are:

The right to a useful and remunerative job in the industries or shops or farms or mines of the nation.

The right of every farmer to raise and sell his products at a return which will give him and his family a decent living.

The right of every business man, large and small, to trade in an atmosphere of freedom from unfair competition and domination by monopolies at home or abroad.

The right of every family to a decent home.

The right to adequate medical care and the opportunity to achieve and enjoy good health.

The right to adequate protection from the economic fears of old age, sickness, accident and unemployment.

The right to a good education.

Message to Congress, 1944

OUR TASK

To win this war wholeheartedly, unequivocally and as quickly as we can is our task of the first importance. To win this war in such a way that there will be no further world wars in the foreseeable future is our second objective. To provide occupations, and to provide a decent standard of living for our men in the armed forces after the war, and for all Americans, are the final objectives.

Accepting the Presidential Nomination, 1944

AFFIRMATION OF STRENGTH

I think that the victory of the American people and their allies in this war will be far more than a victory against fascism and reaction and the dead hand of despotism of the past. The victory of the American people and their allies in this war will be a victory for democracy. It will constitute such an affirmation of the strength and power and vitality of government by the people as history has never before witnessed.

Washington, 1944

DEBT TO POSTERITY

We must, and I hope we will, continue to be united with our allies in a powerful world organization which is ready and able to keep the peace, if necessary by force. To provide that assurance of international security is the policy, the effort and the obligation of this Administration. We owe it to our posterity, we owe it to our heritage of freedom, we owe it to our God, to devote the rest of our lives and all of our capabilities to the building of a solid, durable structure of world peace.

Washington, 1944

A MATURE AMERICA

We are not fighting for, and we shall not attain, a Utopia. Indeed, in our own land, the work to be done is never finished. We have yet to realize the full and equal enjoyment of our freedom. So, in embarking on the building of a world-fellowship, we have set ourselves a long and arduous task, a task which will challenge our patience, our intelligence, our imagination, as well as our faith.

That task calls for the judgment of a seasoned and mature people. This, I think, the American people have become. We shall not again be thwarted in our will to live as a mature nation, confronting limitless horizons. We shall bear our full responsibility, exercise our full influence, and bring our full help and encouragement to all who aspire to peace and freedom.

New York, 1944

THE COMING BATTLE FOR PEACE

Peace, peace no less than war, must offer a spirit of comradeship, a spirit of achievement, a spirit of unselfishness, and indomitable will to victory. We, we in this country for generations have waged war against the wilderness—against the mountains and the rivers—against droughts and storms. We waged war against ignorance, against oppression, against intolerance. We waged war against poverty, against disease. Why, we fought the Revolutionary War for the principle that all men are created equal—and in those days we pledged "our lives, our fortunes, and our sacred honor."

This war which we are now fighting has been an interruption in our forward progress, but it has also opened a new chapter—a chapter which it is now for us, living, to begin.

I say we must wage the coming battle for America and for civilization on a scale worthy of the way we have unitedly waged the battles against tyranny and reaction and wage it through all the difficulties and the disappointments that may ever clog the wheels of progress.

And I say we must wage it in association with the United Nations with whom we have stood and fought —with that association ever growing.

Boston, 1944

MEN, NOT OSTRICHES

We have learned that we can not live alone, at peace; that our own well-being is dependent upon the well-being of other nations, far away. We have learned that we must live as men, and not as ostriches, nor as dogs in the manger. We have learned to be citizens of the world, members of the human community. We have learned the simple truth, as Emerson said, that "the only way to have a friend is to be one." We can gain no lasting peace if we approach it with suspicion and distrust—or with fear. We can gain it only if we proceed with the understanding and the confidence and the courage which flow from conviction.

Fourth Inaugural Address, 1945

PLAN FOR HUMANITY

For the second time in the lives of most of us, this generation is face to face with the objective of preventing wars. To meet that objective, the nations of the world will either have a plan or they will not. The groundwork of a plan has now been furnished, and has been submitted to humanity for discussion and decision.

No plan is perfect. Whatever is adopted at San Francisco will doubtless have to be amended time and again over the years, just as our own Constitution has been.

I am confident that the Congress and the American people will accept the results of this conference as the beginning of a permanent structure of peace upon which we can begin to build, under God, that better world in which our children and grandchildren, yours and mine, the children and grandchildren of the whole world must live and can live.

Report on the Crimea Conference, 1945

ONE WORLD

It is easy for you and me to shrug our shoulders and

to say that conflicts taking place thousands of miles from the continental United States, and indeed thousands of miles from the whole American Hemisphere, do not seriously affect the Americas—and that all the United States has to do is to ignore them and go about its own business. Passionately though we may desire detachment, we are forced to realize that every word that comes through the air, every ship that sails the sea, every battle that is fought does affect the American future.

Talk to the Nation, 1939

CHRONOLOGY OF AN ACTIVE LIFE

FRANKLIN DELANO ROOSEVELT

1882 January 30th —Born at Hyde Park, New York.
1904 —Graduated from Harvard.
1905 March 17th —Married Anna Eleanor Roosevelt.
1910 —Elected to the senate of New York State, his first public office.
1913 —Appointed Assistant Secretary of the Navy.
1920 —Democratic nominee for the Vice-Presidency, as running mate of James M. Cox, both being defeated.
1921 August —Stricken with infantile paralysis.
1928 November 6th—Elected Governor of New York State.
1932 November 8th—Elected President of the United States.
1933 March 4th —Inaugurated President.
1936 November 3rd—Elected to a second term.
1937 January 20th —Inaugurated for a second term, the first President to take office on the new date specified by the Twentieth Amendment.
1940 November 5th—Elected to a third term, shattering a precedent as old as the United States.
1941 January 20th —Inaugurated for a third term.
1941 January —Enunciated the Four Freedoms.
1941 August —Met Prime Minister Churchill at sea.
1941 August 14th —Issued, jointly with Prime Minister Winston Churchill of Great Britain, an eight-point statement of principles of peace which became known as the Atlantic Charter.
1941 December 8th—Appeared before a joint session of Congress and asked that war against Japan be declared.

1943 January	—Met Prime Minister Churchill at Casablanca, the first time a President of the United States had left this country in wartime.
1943 August	—Met Prime Minister Churchill at Quebec.
1943 November	—Conferred at Teheran, Iran, with Prime Minister Churchill and Marshal Stalin.
1944 July	—Went to Pearl Harbor for a conference with General Douglas MacArthur.
1944 November 7th	—Elected to a fourth term as President.
1945 January 20th	—Inaugurated at a simple ceremony.
1945 Feb. 4th-11th	—Conferred at Yalta, Crimea, with Marshal Stalin and Prime Minister Churchill.
1945 April 12th	—Died at Warm Springs, Georgia.
1945 April 15th	—Buried at Hyde Park, New York.

OBJECTIVE READING QUESTIONS

CHAPTER ONE

Choose the correct alternative from among those listed.

1. Roosevelt had _____ (a. one sister   b. a half sister c. a half brother).

2. His mother _____ (a. married a man younger than she b. married twice   c. married a man nearly twice her age).

3. The Roosevelts and the Delanos were _____ (a. rivals b. neighbors   c. enemies).

4. The first Roosevelt came to New York State in _____ (a. 1644   b. 1756   c. 1882).

5. The Roosevelts made _____ their permanent home. (a. New York City   b. Hyde Park   c. New Amsterdam).

6. The home was _____ (a. near the Hudson   b. accessible only by boat   c. at the bottom of a steep hill).

7. Cleveland's wish for Franklin was that _____ (a. he'd become President   b. he'd never be President   c. he'd support him in his next campaign).

8. Marksman was the name of _____ (a. Roosevelt's chum b. his horse   c. his dog).

9. Which of the following is *not* mentioned as one of Roosevelt's hobbies? (a. stamp collecting   b. building boats c. collecting coins).

10. Very early in life Roosevelt showed the qualities of _____ (a. an expert fencer   b. a leader   c. a courageous follower).

CHAPTER TWO

Tell whether each statement is true or false.

1. The Roosevelt estate consisted of more than 1000 acres of land.

2. His chum and he once built a sailboat in a tree.

3. Mrs. Roosevelt forbade Franklin to climb trees.

4. Franklin's father bought him a gun even before Mrs. Roosevelt was willing.
5. Roosevelt killed birds principally for food.
6. His parents had confidence that Franklin could take care of himself.
7. Mrs. Roosevelt had once lived in China.
8. On his trip through Europe Franklin exceeded his daily allowance of money.
9. Franklin had always planned to enter West Point.
10. Mr. Roosevelt wanted Franklin to take over his business eventually.

CHAPTER THREE

Complete each of the following statements.

1. The name of the preparatory school to which Franklin was sent is _____.
2. The foreign languages which Franklin spoke fluently were _____ and _____.
3. At school he managed the _____ team.
4. During the _____ War Franklin planned to join the Navy.
5. The boys were prevented from enlisting by getting a case of _____.
6. The fixed allowance at school was _____ per week.
7. The name of the island where the Roosevelts spent their vacation is _____.
8. Franklin's father joined the _____ Party during the Civil War.
9. Franklin was an editor of the college newspaper, named _____.
10. The name of Franklin's college is _____.

CHAPTER FOUR

Tell whether each statement is true or false.

1. Franklin's bride was older than he.

2. A very important guest at the wedding was President Theodore Roosevelt.
3. They were married on St. Valentine's Day.
4. Their first child was James Roosevelt.
5. Franklin was interested in reforestation.

CHAPTER FIVE

Choose the correct alternative from among those listed.

1. _____ urged Franklin to enter politics. (a. his father b. President Roosevelt   c. his wife).
2. He was nominated for _____ (a. state assemblyman b. state senator   c. U. S. senator).
3. The leader of Tammany Hall _____ (a. predicted Roosevelt's future greatness   b. was happy over Roosevelt's running   c. tried to shoot Roosevelt).
4. Roosevelt was nicknamed _____ (a. the father of the assembly   b. the baby of the senate   c. the incorruptible old man).
5. At this time Roosevelt made a very dear friend named _____ (a. Big Tim   b. Grover Cleveland   c. Al Smith).

CHAPTER SIX

Match items in Column B with those in Column A. There will be one left over.

A	B
1. Franklin D. Roosevelt	A. A destroyer
2. Woodrow Wilson	B. Secretary of the Navy
3. Josephus Daniels	C. A chief of one of the Allies
4. General Scott	D. A huge passenger boat
5. F-4	E. Had appendicitis
6. England	F. Army Chief of Staff
7. Leviathan	G. Wartime President
8. Clemenceau	H. A submarine
9. League of Nations	I. Visited by Roosevelt

10. Mrs. Roosevelt   J. Supported by Roosevelt
                                  and Wilson
                               K. A good wartime home
                                  manager

CHAPTER SEVEN

Complete each of the following statements.

1. The 1920 Democratic convention chose _____ to run
   for President.
2. _____ was chosen to run for Vice-President.
3. The two Republican candidates were _____ and _____.
4. Roosevelt, after the election, returned to the practice of
   _____.
5. He was elected Trustee of _____.

CHAPTER EIGHT

Tell whether each statement is true or false.

1. Roosevelt developed infantile paralysis the year after the
   Presidential election.
2. The attack came after a swim in icy water.
3. Roosevelt was very much depressed at his bad luck.
4. He enjoyed collecting stamps and ship models.
5. Louis Howe gave up an excellent business position to
   stay with Roosevelt.
6. Roosevelt first heard about Warm Springs from Louis
   Howe.
7. For a paralytic, water exercise is more difficult than exercise on land.
8. Roosevelt bought Warm Springs from a man named Peabody.
9. Al Smith nominated Roosevelt for the Presidency in 1924.
10. The "Happy Warrior" refers to Roosevelt.

CHAPTER NINE

Choose the correct alternative from among those listed.

1. Al Smith begged Roosevelt to run for   (a. President
   b. Governor of Georgia   c. Governor of New York).
2. Roosevelt at first refused because of _____ (a. personal
   dislike   b. health   c. finances).
3. At last Roosevelt agreed to _____ (a. seek the nomination   b. run if nominated   c. support Smith as a candidate for Congress).
4. The results of the election were that _____ (a. Smith
   and Roosevelt both won   b. both lost   c. Roosevelt
   won, while Smith lost).
5. The importance of the election was that _____
   (a. Roosevelt became more despondent   b. Roosevelt
   returned to public life   c. the family was united).

CHAPTER TEN

Tell whether each statement is true or false.

1. Many governors of New York State have become presidents of the United States.
2. Roosevelt was interested in reforms that would better the
   lot of the people.
3. Roosevelt often declared that he disliked political fights.
4. Because of his paralysis Roosevelt seldom left Albany.
5. Mrs. Roosevelt enjoyed teaching while she was the Governor's wife.
6. Franklin Roosevelt disliked the idea of running for a
   second term as Governor.
7. Roosevelt was in worse physical shape than most men his
   age, according to the life-insurance doctor.
8. The Warm Springs patients were able to raise only $25.00
   for his campaign.
9. Warm Springs accommodated more than 200 patients in
   1930.   ,

Chapter Eleven

Complete each of the following statements.

1. Roosevelt's decision to run for President disappointed
   _____.

2. Roosevelt's political beliefs were summed up in the phrase
   _____

3. The 1932 Democratic Convention was held in _____.
4. He went from Albany to the Convention by _____.
5. The Republicans nominated _____.

Chapter Twelve

Tell whether each statement is true or false.

1. Roosevelt tried to work long hours, but his ailment prevented him from doing so.
2. Roosevelt was President of the United States at 51.
3. Roosevelt was wounded by a madman's bullet at Miami.
4. All in all, three people were wounded at the parade for Roosevelt.
5. Many banks closed before Roosevelt took office.
6. During the last few months of his term President Hoover acted in close consultation with Franklin D. Roosevelt.
7. After the trouble in Miami, Roosevelt scarcely slept through anxiety.
8. Mr. Cermack was mayor of Miami.
9. Roosevelt spent his 51st birthday at Warm Springs.
10. Between January 1 and March 4 Roosevelt was neither Governor nor President.

Chapter Thirteen

Match items in Column B with those in Column A. There will be one left over.

A	B
1. Franklin D. Roosevelt	A. Close friend, whose death saddened Roosevelt

2. President Hoover
3. John Nance Garner
4. Sarah Delano Roosevelt

5. James Roosevelt
6. Justice Hughes
7. Madam Perkins
8. Douglas MacArthur

9. Justice Cardozo
10. Louis McHenry Howe

B. Chief Justice of Supreme Court
C. Roosevelt's wife
D. First woman Cabinet member
E. Originated "fireside chats"
F. Army chief of staff in 1932
G. Sworn in as Vice-President
H. Rode with Roosevelt at Inauguration
I. Roosevelt's mother
J. Escorted Roosevelt down the runway
K. Associate Justice of Supreme Court

CHAPTER FOURTEEN

Match items in Column B with those in Column A. There will be one left over.

A	B
1. arms embargo	A. surrendered in June
2. Germany	B. a 300-mile zone
3. Canada	C. attacked Poland in September
4. Cordell Hull	D. visited the Roosevelts in 1939
5. Sumner Welles	E. American Minister to Poland
6. "safety belt"	F. restriction on exports
7. George VI	G. included in America's defense plans
8. "flying fortress"	H. small pursuit plane
9. Anthony Biddle	I. represented the U. S. at Lima
10. France	J. Under-Secretary of State
	K. huge airplane

CHAPTER FIFTEEN

Choose the correct alternative from among those listed.

1. _____ was selected to run for the Vice-Presidency.
   (a. James M. Cox   b. Henry A. Wallace   c. William
   G. McAdoo).

2. The President is also _____ (a. Chief of Staff of the
   Army.   b. Commander in Chief of the Army and Navy
   c. Rear Admiral).

3. _____ was Roosevelt's opponent in the 1940 campaign.
   (a. Dewey   b. Willkie   c. Hoover).

4. Roosevelt always voted in _____ (a. Hyde Park
   b. Washington   c. Albany).

5. Roosevelt was the first American President to win _____
   (a. a two-million plurality   b. all the electoral votes but
   42   c. a third term).

6. The Speaker of the House of Representatives was named
   _____ (a. Hughes   b. Rayburn   c. Garner).

7. The Bible used for the inauguration oath belonged to
   _____ (a. Roosevelt's family   b. The Supreme Court
   c. The Capitol).

8. "Old Man Commonsense" was Roosevelt's name for _____
   (a. Garner   b. Wallace   c. Hughes).

9. After the parade _____ were invited to tea at the White
   House. (a. 1000   b. 2500   c. 40).

10. "I love a good fight" was a famous statement by _____
    (a. Al Smith   b. Wallace   c. Roosevelt).

CHAPTER SIXTEEN

Tell whether each statement is true or false.

1. Interviews with President Roosevelt were planned for
   fifteen minutes each.

2. Roosevelt seldom kept his visitors beyond the allotted time.

3. Roosevelt always had lunch at a favorite restaurant, not
   far from the Washington Monument.

4. Roosevelt often carried on the business of state even while
   swimming.

5. Roosevelt enjoyed occasional week-ends at Hyde Park.
6. The gap left by Louis Howe's death was filled by Harry Hopkins.
7. Harry Hopkins disagreed with the President on nearly every matter of importance.
8. Fala was Roosevelt's pet German shepherd dog.
9. The Monroe Doctrine was formulated about 1875.
10. Roosevelt renounced the Monroe Doctrine.

CHAPTER SEVENTEEN
Complete each of the following statements.

The Four Freedoms as set down by President Roosevelt are:
1. _____
2. _____
3. _____
4. _____
5. The European country which Roosevelt held up as a warning of what might happen was _____.
6. Roosevelt declared that spies and their agents were already here and in _____.
7. He asked for immediate increase in _____.
8. He thought America should support _____ by sending them supplies.
9. A quotation from _____ magazine is included in the chapter.
10. The famous speech was delivered in _____ 1941.

CHAPTER EIGHTEEN
Match items in Column B with those in Column A. There will be one left over.

A	B
1. Winston Churchill	A. an officer in the Marines
2. George Marshall	B. British battleship
3. Elliott Roosevelt	C. British naval officer
4. Augusta	D. a Roosevelt present at the signing of the Atlantic Charter
5. Prince of Wales	
6. Ernest J. King	

7. H. H. Arnold
8. Mrs. John Boettiger
9. James Roosevelt
10. Admiral Leahy

E. the eldest of the Roosevelt children
F. co-signer of the Atlantic Charter
G. Chief of Staff of Army
H. Chief of Naval Operations
I. American cruiser
J. Head of Army Air Forces
K. Roosevelt's aide

CHAPTER NINETEEN

Complete each of the following statements.

The "big three" during the war were:

1. _____.
2. _____.
3. _____.
4. _____ then commanded the American forces fighting in North Africa.
5. He later became _____ in Europe.

The two world leaders who met in Casablanca were:

6. _____.
7. _____.
8. For their meeting in Canada the two leaders chose the city of _____.
9. At Cairo another world leader joined the conference; his name, _____.
10. At Teheran still another world leader conferred; his name, _____.

CHAPTER TWENTY

Match items in Column B with those in Column A. There will be one left over.

<table>
<tr><td align="center">A</td><td align="center">B</td></tr>
<tr><td>1. Harry Truman</td><td>A. senator from Missouri</td></tr>
<tr><td>2. Thomas Dewey</td><td>B. ruler of Ethiopia</td></tr>
<tr><td>3. Mrs. Boettiger</td><td>C. ruler of Egypt</td></tr>
</table>

4. San Francisco	D. candidate for Presidency in 1944
5. Yalta	
6. King Farouk	E. watched over father's health
7. Ibn Saud	
8. Haile Selassie	F. place of U. N.'s first meeting
9. Admiral Ross McIntyre	
10. Edward Stettinius	G. Secretary of State
	H. Army Chief of Staff
	I. site of historic "big three" conference
	J. ruler of Arabia
	K. Roosevelt's physician

Chapter Twenty-One

Tell whether each statement is true or false.

1. Roosevelt had been ill several days before his death.
2. His death was attributed to overwork.
3. Mrs. Roosevelt had had a hint of her husband's approaching death.
4. Several days after the death of President Roosevelt, Harry Truman was sworn in as the new President.
5. Once again Chief Justice Hughes swore in the President of the United States.
6. All the Roosevelt children were able to come home for the funeral services.
7. Roosevelt was mourned by persons in far-off lands as well as by Americans.
8. President Roosevelt was buried in Arlington Memorial Cemetery.
9. The services were lengthy, taking more than an hour and a half.
10. Bishop Dunn, in his tribute to Roosevelt, quoted the President's words about fear.